COOL LAYER CAKES

50 DELICIOUS AND AMAZING LAYER CAKES TO BAKE AND DECORATE

CERI OLOFSON

APPLE

A QUINTET BOOK

First published 2014 in the UK by
Apple Press
74-77 White Lion Street
London N1 9PF
United Kingdom

www.apple-press.com

ISBN: 978-1-8454-3523-3

QTT:CLCA

Project Editor: Salima Hirani
Designer: Lucy Parissi
Photographers: Ria Osborne &
Clare Winfield
Food Stylist: Ceri Olofson
Art Director: Michael Charles
Assistant Art Director: Tania
Gomes
Editorial Director: Emma Bastow
Publisher: Mark Searle

Printed in China by Shanghai
Offset Printing Products Ltd.

9 8 7 6 5 4 3 2 1

NOTE: all oven temperatures in
this book are for fan ovens. If
using a non-fan oven, increase
the temperature by 20 degrees.

CONTENTS

INTRODUCTION

A layer cake in its simplest form consists of multiple layers of cake and filling. What sets it apart from a sandwich cake is that it has a minimum of three layers (the clue is in the name, after all). When you start stacking up those layers, even the humblest cake is transformed into something special. In the case of layer cakes, bigger is better, as it allows more opportunity for packing in flavour and, also, creating impactful designs is easier with a tall bake. So, start building your cakes high for drama and visual appeal.

We've all enjoyed layer cakes at some point. They make the perfect addition to many social gatherings, from catching up with old friends over coffee and celebrating a new job to the big wedding day. Nothing beats sharing a gorgeous, delicious cake with loved ones, so why not make each gathering a little bit more special with a spectacular treat?

With so many excuses to make cakes comes the opportunity to try variations on a theme. This book begins with a section that looks at the foundations of making layer cakes and includes a repertoire of core recipes that you can modify with your own chosen flavours, as well as ideas to encourage you to think about interesting flavour combinations, much as you would use a colour palette to consider pleasing colour combinations. Being a wedding cake designer and self-taught cake decorator, I know how important it is to get the basics of layering and frosting right. If your cake is stable and well put together, it is much easier to decorate it well, so I provide information on a variety of essential techniques in this section.

Next in the book come the cake projects themselves, beginning with a section on indulgent feel-good treats that are designed to make a cup of tea and slice of cake much more special. Following this is a section dedicated to cakes with a surprise – a hidden wow factor – because what's on the inside should be beautiful, too. After this section come the cakes designed to mark important occasions of all sorts and to enliven parties with a bit of confection dazzle. Last of all come the showstoppers, for those memorable events when you want something super special.

In the sections on cake projects, the focus shifts toward decorating and, as you progress through the projects the complexity advances, so you begin by learning simple sugarcraft techniques and, by the end of the book, you will be able to make a small tiered showstopper! I've included projects that use a variety of techniques without requiring lots of specialist materials and also show how fantastic cake designs can be created with a little imagination and minimal supplies. Throughout, I encourage you to modify the cake designs once you feel confident enough to do so. Make each design your own, and let the projects in this book inspire you. Change the colour schemes, combine details from various projects, use buttercream frosting instead of fondant, switch flavours from vanilla to chocolate simply because it's your favourite… Use the projects and recipes as a springboard for your own ideas. I hope that this book will give you the confidence to take your layer cakes to new heights!

CERI OLOFSON

LAYER CAKE ESSENTIALS

ESSENTIAL TOOLS

Below is my advice on the tools you'll need to make awesome layer cakes. With some basic items, creating amazing results becomes simple once you've mastered the skills. Using quality equipment will make life easier, so buy the best you can. These are the tools I couldn't live without.

Bowls These should be heatproof, ideally. I like to use glass, ceramic or plastic bowls as metal cannot be used in the microwave and tends to conduct heat. Choose a nesting set of bowls to save space and make sure the sides are fairly deep. Breakfast cereal-size bowls are useful for mixing colour into small quantities of batter or frosting.

Cooling racks These aid in the cooling of cake layers as they allow air to circulate around the cake and avoid steam building up in any areas, which would lead to soggy edges.

Electric handheld whisk This relatively mobile tool is good for whipping up small quantities.

Electric stand mixer A stand mixer can cream butter until it is fluffy as a cloud, and makes it easy to blend large quantities. Some recipes almost rely on the ability to leave the stand mixer running, such as the Italian Meringue Buttercream (see page 14). However, in most cases you can simply use an electric handheld whisk instead, but be prepared to work it for longer to get similar results.

Cake tins Look for straight-sided tins that are at least 7.5 cm (3 in) deep. To make layer cakes you will need a minimum of two tins, but three is better and will save you a lot of time. All the recipes in this book are based on 20-cm (8-in) round tins unless otherwise stated, but if you want to use square tins or tins of different sizes, refer to the cake-scaling guide on page 10.

Oven thermometer Most ovens vary in temperature, so an oven thermometer will ensure consistent results.

Silicone spatulas Use these to scrape down the sides of bowls and to make sure that all the ingredients in a mixture are well combined. Because they are efficient at clearing bowl contents, there is less left in the bowl to wash up.

Knives You'll need a long serrated knife for cutting and carving cakes, and a sharp paring knife for trimming fondant.

Measuring spoons Accurate measuring spoons make the difference between a perfect rise and a dense mess when it comes to measuring ingredients such as baking powder. A nesting set of metal spoons is ideal.

Electronic scales A set of electronic scales will revolutionise your baking. Most use various units of measurement, which allows you to weigh liquids as well as dry ingredients. Being able to place the mixing bowl directly on the scale, reset the scale, and add ingredients as you go is a time-saving and accurate way of measuring ingredients for baking.

Parchment paper Parchment paper is used for lining cake tins and is also useful for practising piping over a template design.

Pastry brush A pastry brush is used for brushing cakes with sugar syrup as well as buttering tins. A brush with bristles is preferable to the silicone variety as it picks up more of the syrup/ingredient.

ESSENTIAL DECORATING KIT

Cake boards Boards come in a variety of shapes and sizes. They are often made of strong cardboard covered in wax paper. Use one underneath your cake so that you can move it around more easily. Either choose one that is the same size as your cake or opt for one a few centimetres larger and make a feature of it. But if you do so, make sure you cover the paper with frosting or decoration – nothing spoils a beautiful cake faster than an unfinished cake board!

Food colouring Food colouring pastes or gels offer intense, concentrated spots of colour. As a general rule, add a little colour at a time until you reach the required shade. Liquid colours make fondant sticky and are not strong, so pastes are the way to go for all applications, including baking.

Paintbrushes Paintbrushes can be used to add embellishments to decorations, as well as to brush away icing sugar and cake crumbs. Make sure you keep a dedicated baking set separate from other paintbrushes and wash them well after each use.

Piping bags These are made from reusable fabric or disposable plastic, and you can make your own from wax paper for small projects. Disposable bags are convenient but not environmentally friendly. If you are stuck, you can use a zipped bag with a corner cut off, but the results won't be as reliable as those achieved when using a piping bag.

Sprinkles Sprinkles provide a quick way of jazzing up a cake. They are generally made of sugar and come in a staggering variety of colours and designs.

Scissors You'll need a good pair of scissors for cutting fondant and gum paste, as well as for other baking jobs. It's worth keeping a clean, sharp pair separate from your general paper scissors.

Scalpel A super-sharp scalpel is useful for cutting out templates and any design that needs some precision. Keep it separate from your general-use scalpels.

Fondant cutters Cutters are available in a wide variety of designs and sizes. They are much like biscuit cutters but are made from a nonstick plastic and sometimes include an extra embossing stamp. Cutters offer a very easy way of adding extra decoration to a cake.

Turntable A turntable makes it easier to move around the sides of your cake, which helps when smoothing frosting or piping decoration. It also lifts up the cake, bringing it closer to eye level, which is also useful when decorating.

SPECIAL TOOLS

Cake leveller A cake leveller is a metal frame with a serrated wire pulled across, and with notches that allow you to adjust the height. This tool is the wedding cake maker's secret weapon because it makes it so easy to create flat, level cake layers. You can use a serrated knife, but a leveller ensures an even cut all the way through the cake. This tool will take your cakes to a whole new professional 'level!'

Sugar thermometer The idea of dealing with the different stages of hot sugar can be an intimidating thought, but a sugar thermometer takes the uncertainty out of the process, opening up new recipe possibilities. For example, Italian Meringue Buttercream (see page 14) uses molten sugar to cook the meringue, which would not be possible to achieve without a thermometer.

Cake-release spray There is nothing wrong with lining and greasing cake tins in the conventional way, but if you can get your hands on some cake-release spray or fluid, which is usually comprised of a super-slick oil, you will never worry about cakes sticking again. It can make preparing tins a cinch.

Dough scraper Although designed for use with dough, a dough scraper is actually the key to amazingly smooth and straight frosted sides on cakes. Dragged around a frosted cake, a dough scraper will help you to create a smooth finish and produce a perfect right angle between the cake sides and the tabletop surface.

Angled metal spatula Angled spatulas have a cranked handle, so using one gives you a better angle when applying frosting. They are also useful for picking up decorations, slicing fondant and loosening cakes in their tins. It is helpful to have small, medium and large angled spatulas on hand for different projects.

Nonstick fondant rolling pin Fondant rolling pins are made of a very smooth nonstick plastic and are indispensable as wooden pins leave marks. Mini pins are good for rolling out small amounts of fondant or gum paste for decorating, whereas you will need a much larger pin for covering a whole cake. If necessary, a silicone, ceramic or glass pin can be substituted.

Fondant smoothers These nifty tools will take your finish from passable to pro with very little effort! The flat plastic paddles have handles that make it easy to glide the tools over the fondant-covered cake, smoothing as they go and evening out the surface. Fondant smoothers also help to ensure the fondant is 'fixed' to the cake underneath, as the pressure bonds the layers together.

BASIC CAKE RECIPES

These recipes provide the perfect consistencies for layering cakes so you can rely on them to take the stress out of baking, allowing you to apply your energies to creativity and decoration skills. You can call on these recipes in endless combinations as you play with your ideas. Use the best-quality ingredients you can – they will serve you well.

THE CAKES

All of the cake recipes in this section produce a single 20-cm (8-in) cake layer that is between 5 and 10 cm (2 and 4 in) deep, so you simply need to multiply the recipe quantities by the number of layers you want and split the batter between as many tins. These core recipes are used in the projects throughout the book and the quantity of cake batter needed (for the same number of layers required for the cake project) is stated in the ingredients list for each project. Once cooled, each of these cakes can be kept in an airtight container for up to one week.

CAKE SCALING GUIDE

CAKE TIN SIZE	MULTIPLY RECIPE BY
15 cm (6 in)	½
18 cm (7 in)	¾
20 cm (8 in)	1
23 cm (9 in)	1½
25 cm (10 in)	2
28 cm (11 in)	2½
30 cm (12 in)	3¼
35 cm (14 in)	4¼

Ultimate Sponge Cake

Fluffy and buttery, this sponge can be flavoured in a myriad of ways. At the end, add 1 tsp vanilla extract, the zest of half a lemon or orange, 1 tsp espresso powder or ½ tsp rose extract; the options are endless.

200 g (7 oz) caster sugar
200 g (7 oz) unsalted butter, softened
4 large eggs
200 g (7 oz) self-raising flour
Flavouring of your choice

Preheat the oven to 160°C (325°F). Grease a 20-cm (8-in) round cake tin and line it with parchment paper. Alternatively, spray the tin with cake-release spray.

In the large bowl of an electric stand mixer, beat together the sugar and butter until very pale and fluffy.

In a mixing bowl, lightly beat the eggs. Slowly add the beaten eggs to the sugar and butter mixture with the stand mixer running on a medium speed.

Once combined, add the flour and mix at low speed until just combined. Gently fold in your chosen flavouring until it is blended into the batter.

Spread the batter into the prepared cake tin and bake for 45–50 minutes. You will know that the sponge cake is cooked when the sides are coming away from the tin and a cocktail stick inserted into the centre of the cake comes out clean.

Allow the cake to cool in the tin for 20 minutes, then transfer to a cooling rack to cool completely.

Chocolate Fudge Cake

This cake is unapologetically dense, moist and chocolatey. The coffee enhances the flavour yet is virtually undetectable in the final cake, but you can use decaffeinated coffee or hot water if you prefer. Add 2 drops of peppermint extract or the grated zest of half an orange with 1 tsp of orange extract for mint chocolate and orange chocolate variations. Replace the flour with a gluten-free flour blend for a wheat-free version.

200 g (7 oz) caster sugar
2 large eggs
140 g (5 oz) sour cream
120 ml (4 fl oz) sunflower oil
165 g (5¾ oz) plain flour
55 g (2 oz) unsweetened cocoa powder
1 tsp baking powder
Pinch of salt
150 ml (5 fl oz) hot coffee
50 g (1¾ oz) plain or dark chocolate, chopped
1 tsp vanilla extract

Preheat the oven to 160°C (350°F). Grease a 20-cm (8-in) round cake tin and line it with parchment paper. Alternatively, spray the tin with cake-release spray.

In the large bowl of an electric stand mixer, beat together the sugar and eggs until the mixture is thick and pale. Then beat in the sour cream, followed by the oil.

In a separate bowl, sieve together the flour, cocoa powder, baking powder and salt. Add the dry ingredients to the wet mixture in the stand mixer bowl and mix to make a dough.

In a separate bowl, pour the hot coffee over the chocolate and stir until the chocolate has melted. Add the vanilla extract, then pour the hot liquid into the mixture in the bowl of the stand mixer while the machine is running on a medium speed until the ingredients are combined. Scrape down the sides of the bowl with a silicone spatula and mix fully.

Pour the batter into the prepared tin and bake for 60 to 70 minutes. Allow to cool in the tin for 20 minutes, then transfer to a cooling rack to cool completely.

Red Velvet Cake

This is everything a red velvet cake should be – moist, subtly balanced between vanilla and chocolate and, most importantly, very red! The secret is using red food colouring paste and a little goes a long way, so just add a modest amount to start with as you can always increase the intensity as you go. You can also use natural food colouring, but be aware that the colour will never be as intense as when using a paste.

150 g (5½ oz) caster sugar
60 g (2¼ oz) unsalted butter, softened
1 large egg
120 ml (4 fl oz) buttermilk
1 tsp vanilla extract
Red food colouring paste
20 g (¾ oz) unsweetened cocoa powder
150 g (5½ oz) plain flour
½ tsp baking soda
1½ tsp white vinegar

Preheat the oven to 160°C (350°F). Grease a 20-cm (8-in) round cake tin and line it with parchment paper. Alternatively, spray the cake tin with cake-release spray.

In the large bowl of an electric stand mixer, beat together the sugar and butter until the mixture is light and fluffy.

In a separate bowl, lightly beat the egg. Slowly add the beaten egg to the sugar and butter mixture with the stand mixer running on a medium speed.

In a separate small bowl, mix together the buttermilk, vanilla and red food colouring paste until the buttermilk takes on an intense red colour. You can add more colouring paste later if the mix doesn't look colourful enough.

Sieve together the cocoa powder and flour in a separate bowl.

With the stand mixer running on a low speed, add half the red buttermilk to the butter mixture, followed by half the flour and cocoa mixture. Repeat this process until all the

buttermilk and flour mixture have been added, scraping down the sides of the bowl with a spatula between additions.

Add the baking soda and vinegar and beat until well mixed and smooth. At this point you can add more red colouring if needed. Pour the batter into the prepared cake tin and bake for 30–35 minutes.

Allow the cake to cool in the tin for 20 minutes, then transfer to a cooling rack to cool completely.

Carrot Cake

This cake is full of flavour and very moist, and you can almost convince yourself that it is good for you with all those grated carrots. Wonderfully light, this sponge cake can be adapted to your taste by changing the nuts and spice mix. I love the flavour of orange zest with the warm spices. I add my own Swedish-inspired twist by including ground cardamom and a dash of ground black pepper for extra warmth.

200 g (7 oz) light brown sugar
2 large eggs
200 ml (7 fl oz) sunflower oil
200 g (7 oz) plain flour
½ tsp baking soda
½ tsp baking powder
1 tsp pumpkin pie spice
½ tsp ground cinnamon
½ tsp ground ginger
½ tsp ground cardamom (optional)
2 pinches of ground black pepper (optional)
2 pinches of salt
200 g (7 oz) carrots, grated
60 g (2¼ oz) pecans, walnuts or hazelnuts, chopped
Grated zest of 1 orange

Preheat the oven to 160°C (350°F). Grease a 20-cm (8-in) round cake tin and line it with parchment paper. Alternatively, spray the cake tin with cake-release spray.

Place the sugar, egg and oil in the large bowl of an electric stand mixer and beat together until well combined.

Slowly add the flour, baking soda, baking powder, ground spices and salt and continue to beat until well mixed.

Stir in the carrots, nuts and orange zest by hand until the mixture is evenly combined.

Spread the cake batter in the prepared cake tin and bake for 20–25 minutes.

Allow the cake to cool in the tin for 20 minutes, then transfer to a cooling rack to cool completely.

Gluten-Free Sponge

This recipe produces a light and airy gluten-free sponge cake that can be flavoured in lots of ways. It is a fat-free recipe, which keeps the texture light and spongy, but make sure that you add double the normal quantities of the flavouring of your choice so that the flavour packs a punch, and always brush the sponge cake with an infused simple syrup (see page 17).

8 large eggs
200 g (7 oz) caster sugar
200 g (7 oz) gluten-free self-raising flour
Flavouring of your choice

Preheat the oven to 160°C (350°F). Grease a 20-cm (8-in) round cake tin and line it with parchment paper. Alternatively, spray the cake tin with cake-release spray.

Place a heatproof mixing bowl over a saucepan of simmering water, making sure the bottom of the bowl does not touch the water.

Place the eggs and sugar in the bowl and, using an electric handheld whisk, whisk until the mixture is thick and mousse-like. It is ready when a ribbon trail is left behind when you lift the whisk out of the bowl.

Using a metal spoon, gently fold in the flour. Mix in your chosen flavouring at this point.

Pour the mixture into the prepared cake tin and bake for 25 minutes.

Allow the cake to cool in the tin for 20 minutes, then transfer to a cooling rack to cool completely.

FROSTING AND SYRUP

All of these frosting recipes yield enough to fill and cover a three-layer 20-cm (8-in) cake. Once on the cake, they will be stable at room temperature for at least three days. The frostings can all be flavoured with extracts, zests, jams and curds. Just add a little at a time to the batter until you achieve the desired flavour intensity.

Classic Buttercream

This is the simplest of the buttercreams, and the sweetest due to the icing sugar it contains. The double cream helps to cut through this and lift the flavour. You can add vanilla extract, grated citrus zest, cooled melted chocolate or jam for flavour, adding your chosen flavouring a little at a time and beating well to incorporate it.

500 g (1 lb 2 oz) unsalted butter, softened
500 g (1 lb 2 oz) icing sugar, sieved
2–4 tbsp double cream

In the large bowl of an electric stand mixer, beat the butter until it is pale. Add half of the sugar and mix it into the butter while the mixer is running on a slow speed. Once combined, add the remaining sugar.

Increase the mixer speed to high and beat the mixture for approximately 5 minutes until it is very light and fluffy.

Reduce the speed of the mixer to medium and add the double cream a little at a time until you achieve a smooth, spreadable consistency.

TIP: When you add the sugar to the beaten butter, wrap a clean kitchen towel tightly around the top of the stand mixer bowl to avoid a cloud of icing sugar turning your kitchen into a snowy Christmas scene.

STORAGE: Keep in an airtight container in the fridge for up to two weeks or freeze for up to one month.

Italian Meringue Buttercream

Velvety, light, faintly sweet and oh, so buttery... Need I go on? I urge you to try this, the queen of buttercreams. Don't be put off by the hot simple syrup element – it really is very easy if you use a sugar thermometer and follow the instructions. You will be rewarded with a superior buttercream that is a dream to pipe with and carries flavour beautifully. You can substitute Classic Buttercream where this Italian Meringue Buttercream is called for if you are short on time.

300 g (10½ oz) caster sugar
100 ml (3½ fl oz) water
165 g (5¾ oz) pasteurised egg whites or 5 large egg whites
500 g (1 lb 2 oz) unsalted butter, softened

Place 250 g (9 oz) of the sugar and the water into a small saucepan. Place a sugar thermometer into the saucepan and set the saucepan over a medium-high heat. Do not stir the sugar and water mixture. Simply leave it to dissolve and bubble.

Once bubbles start to form in the syrup, start whisking the egg whites in the large bowl of a stand mixer set on a medium speed. When they are foamy, gradually add the remaining sugar and continue to whisk until stiff, smooth peaks form.

Once the syrup reaches 130°C (265°F), take the saucepan off the heat and pour it, in a thin stream, into the meringue with the mixer set on a medium-low speed. Work steadily and be very careful as the hot syrup could burn you.

Ganache

This recipe makes a spreadable, firm-setting ganache that is ideal for covering cakes. You can also whip it up once it has cooled to make a lighter cake filling. Use the best chocolate you can find, ideally couverture, which is of the highest quality. Use ganache when it is at room temperature, which is when it is at optimal spreading consistency (the same is true for Classic Buttercream).

For dark chocolate:
600 g (1 lb 5 oz) plain or dark chocolate chips or, if using a block, chopped finely (minimum 53 per cent cocoa solids)
300 ml (10 fl oz) double cream

For white or milk chocolate:
750 g (1 lb 10 oz) white or milk chocolate chips or, if using a block, chopped finely
250 ml (8½ fl oz) double cream

Put the chocolate in a heatproof bowl. Place the cream in a medium saucepan and heat it until it is barely simmering. Pour the hot cream over the chocolate, tap the sides of the bowl and let it all settle for 1–2 minutes.

Gently whisk the chocolate and cream together, then allow to cool until the mixture has a spreadable consistency.

TIP: Ganache is notoriously fickle and prone to separating if overheated or overworked. To avoid this with smaller batches, try the alternative method of placing the chocolate and cream in a glass or ceramic bowl and microwave on a medium heat in short 20-second bursts, allowing the mixture to rest in between bursts. Once the chocolate starts to melt you can gently stir the mixture to even out the melting, but only beat the chocolate and cream together once they are naturally melting into each other.

STORAGE: Keep in an airtight container in the fridge for up to one week or freeze for up to one month and beat back to a smooth consistency before using. Once on the cake, it should keep for as long as the expiration date of the cream.

Once all of the syrup has been poured in, reduce the speed of the mixer to its lowest setting and keep it running until the bowl is cool to the touch. This can take up to 10 minutes.

Now add the butter, in small chunks, slowly, until everything is combined. Keep the mixer running until it comes together to form a smooth buttercream with a spreadable consistency. Now you can add any flavourings or colour you wish to incorporate.

TIP: Don't worry if the mixture looks loose and goopy when you add the butter. Just let the mixer continue and it should come together as the mixture cools down. This is usually because the meringue mixture hasn't cooled enough and it melts the butter, so just let it cool for longer next time.

STORAGE: Keep in an airtight container in the fridge for up to one week or freeze for up to one month and beat back to a smooth consistency before using.

Cream Cheese Frosting

Cream Cheese really helps to cut through the richness of a cake that is on the sweet side, such as Red Velvet (see page 12). Try adding a squeeze of lemon juice at the end for extra freshness.

250 g (9 oz) unsalted butter, softened
500 g (1 lb 2 oz) icing sugar, sieved
250 g (9 oz) full-fat cream cheese, cold

In the large bowl of an electric stand mixer, beat the butter until it is pale.

Add half of the sugar and blend it into the butter with the mixer set on a slow speed. Once they are well combined, add the remaining sugar. If necessary, hold a clean kitchen towel over the bowl of the stand mixer to prevent the powdery icing sugar rising up in a cloud.

Increase the speed of the mixer to high and beat the mixture for approximately 5 minutes until it is very light and fluffy.

Decrease the speed of the mixer to medium and add the cream cheese. Continue to beat the mixture until you achieve a smooth, spreadable consistency.

TIP: Do not use reduced-fat cream cheese as it is too thin, and this frosting should be thick and creamy. The butter is needed in this recipe to give the frosting body and to help stabilise the cream cheese.

STORAGE: Keep in an airtight container in the fridge for up to one week or freeze for up to one month. As this frosting contains fresh cream cheese it needs to be refrigerated once used on the cake and consumed within five days of making.

Royal Icing

Royal icing is a soft paste that sets hard. It is ideal for piping decorations and for using as an edible glue. This recipe makes a relatively large amount, but it is difficult to scale down much beyond these quantities. If you have any left over, pipe decorations onto some wax paper, allow them to dry, and then store them in an airtight container indefinitely, ready to use for last-minute cake projects.

500 g (1 lb 2 oz) icing sugar, sieved
60 g (2¼ oz) pasteurised egg whites
or 2 large fresh egg whites

Place the sugar in the bowl of an electric stand mixer along with about two-thirds of the egg whites and blend together with the mixer set on a low speed. Once they are combined, check the consistency and, if the mixture looks dry and crumbly, add more of the egg white and blend until the mixture is smooth but not wet.

Continue to beat the mixture with the mixer set on a low speed for about 5 minutes until it reaches a firm, stiff peak consistency. At this stage you can alter the consistency and add any colouring (see tip, below).

Cover immediately and keep in an airtight container until ready to use.

TIP: You can alter the consistency of the royal icing by adding a little water. When sticking decorations to a cake, you need it to have a fairly stiff consistency, whereas royal icing for decorative piping requires a more free-flowing, soft peak consistency. If you add too much water, simply mix in some extra icing sugar. Paste food dyes add brilliant colour to the white base. Add a very small amount at a time with a cocktail stick.

STORAGE: Keep in an airtight container in the fridge for up to two weeks.

Simple Syrup

This syrup will add moisture to your cakes and infuse an extra layer of flavour. You want to aim for a light brushing with a pastry brush as too much will result in a soggy sponge. You can flavour the syrup (see box, right) according to taste or recipe requirements.

100 g (3½ oz) caster sugar
100 ml (3½ fl oz) water

Place the sugar and water in a saucepan and bring to the boil. Remove the saucepan from the heat once the sugar has dissolved and the liquid has boiled for 1–2 minutes. Leave to cool.

Once cooled to a warm temperature add flavourings to infuse, ideally overnight in the fridge.

STORAGE: Keep in an airtight container in the fridge for up to two weeks.

FLAVOURING FROSTING AND CAKE BATTER

If you want to flavour cake batter, a frosting or syrup, use 1 tsp of flavour extract or liqueur, the grated zest of one citrus fruit, 1 tsp whole spice (for syrup), 1 tsp ground spice (for batter or frosting), or the seeds from ½ vanilla pod per batch of any recipe. Flavours can all be adapted to suit your own palate, so use this as a starting-off point and flavour to taste.

PREPARATION AND FLAVOUR GUIDELINES

The following tips will help you create delicious sponge cake for your layer cakes. I've also provided a guide to using the recipes in this book, both to make faithful recreations of the cake projects or to change ideas to make them your own.

TIPS FOR SUCCESSFUL BAKING

• I cannot stress enough how important it is to have all of your ingredients at room temperature. This prevents mixtures from splitting and ensures that ingredients combine smoothly. You can always place ingredients in the microwave for very short bursts to help warm them up if necessary. Just be cautious; otherwise you will melt butter and cook eggs!

• The key to stress-free baking is to have all of your equipment and ingredients ready before you start mixing. This means you should weigh everything, prepare cake tins and crack eggs into a bowl. Cracking eggs into a bowl is also handy as you can lightly beat them and when you pour them into your cake mix, any accidental traces of shell usually sink to the bottom.

• Preparing a cake tin is essential in order to prevent the batter from sticking and dragging as it rises in the oven, and to ensure a smooth turn-out of the cooked cake. Grease cake tins with butter or oil, depending on what is used in the recipe and add parchment paper (cut to size) to the bottom of the tin. For larger cakes, add a strip of parchment paper around the greased sides, followed by a piece on the bottom of the tin to help insulate against prolonged baking time.

• Serve all cakes at room temperature, as the fridge hardens fats such as butter and can make the cakes seem dry.

• Cake boards should be the same size as the cake itself (i.e., the same measurement as the cake tin) unless specified in a recipe.

• Use large eggs unless otherwise stated.

• To test if a cake is cooked, insert a cocktail stick into the centre of the cake. If it comes out clean, the cake is cooked. If not, return the cake to the oven for a little while longer and test again.

• Unless otherwise specified, cakes fresh from the oven should be left to cool in the cake tins for 20 minutes, then turned out onto a wire rack and left to cool completely.

USING THE CAKE PROJECT RECIPES

Some of the cake projects in this book provide cake recipes, but most of the projects refer you to the Basic Cake Recipes given on pages 10–13. In most cases, one or more batches of batter will be required, which will then be cooked in a way that differs from the cooking method given in the Basic Cake Recipes section. In that case, the ingredients list for the cake project recipe will state that the batter is required.

In other cases, one or more layers of a particular cake, as prepared in a recipe given in the Basic Cake Recipes section, will be required. The ingredients list for the cake project will state the number of layers required but no

cooking instructions will be provided as you can follow those given in the Basic Cake Recipes section.

In some cases, the shape of the cake layers will be different. For example, a square 20-cm/8-in cake tin might be required rather than a round one of the same size. In this case, you should follow the recipe as given in the Basic Cake Recipes section using the shape of tin specified in the cake project recipe. Use your own judgment when it comes to deciding that a cake has been baked for long enough.

When sponge cake layers of a particular flavour are required, the cake project recipe ingredients list will state the amount of flavouring needed per layer. Mix the flavouring into the batter before pouring it into the tin(s) and baking as directed in this chapter.

Some recipes call for prepared cakes of a particular size. The recipe might state which flavour to use and/or the type of frosting to use, or it leaves it up to you to decide. Select from the Basic Cake Recipes on pages 10–13, or from the additional recipes provided in the Feel-good Treats and Buried Treasure sections, according to your own tastes and requirements, to prepare the cake(s). Then follow the decoration techniques as advised in the cake project recipe method.

FABULOUS FLAVOUR PAIRINGS

The Basic Cake Recipes on pages 10–13 are all adaptable, so you can really experiment with flavour combinations by adding whatever flavourings you want. Here are some of my favourite combinations:

- vanilla sponge cake with berry jam and vanilla buttercream frosting
- chocolate fudge cake with plain or dark chocolate ganache and salted caramel
- carrot cake with orange buttercream frosting
- lemon sponge cake with lemon curd and cream cheese frosting
- cardamom sponge cake with white chocolate ganache
- rose sponge cake with raspberry buttercream frosting and lemon curd

DECORATION KNOW-HOW

There are some basic decorating and preparation techniques that are at the heart of many of the projects in this book. This section is full of useful advice on setting up your cake just right, the differences between frosting types, top tips for a professional finish and troubleshooting.

ALL ABOUT FROSTING

Understanding the differences between the frosting recipes used in this book will help you to decide which is the best one for the job at hand.

Classic buttercream This sweet, soft frosting is robust as it contains a large quantity of icing sugar that holds it together like a paste and makes it stable at room temperature. Buttercream never dries hard but does form a crust, so add decorations such as sprinkles when it has been freshly applied. Classic buttercream is useful for tall cakes or a project that needs a frosting to hold it together.

Italian meringue buttercream Being the least sweet of the soft frosting recipes, this buttercream is great if you find classic buttercream too sweet. It is a good choice for cakes with many layers of filling as it won't compete with those flavours. Silky and light, it is lovely to work with and makes piping and achieving a smooth finish on cakes easy. It never forms a crust and stays soft at room temperature.

Ganache Ganache is the best undercoat for fondant as you can achieve really smooth results that set well. This is especially useful if you are transporting your cake as it provides a little protection against sliding cake layers. White chocolate tastes predominantly of vanilla, so it pairs well with most cake flavours, and you can, of course, add a little extract such as peppermint or lemon zest.

Royal icing This is used mostly for decorative work. Old fashioned wedding cakes were covered in hard, bright white royal icing, but the softness of fondant or frosting is more popular now. You can alter the consistency by adding water or icing sugar for various uses. Royal icing holds its shape when piped and dries to a hard, crunchy texture. It's useful for sticking decorations onto fondant.

Fondant Also known as sugar paste and ready-to-use fondant, this frosting is used to cover cakes in a smooth, pliable layer and for making sugar decorations. It sets but never dries hard, so can be manipulated in many ways. Handling it takes practise and it is best used for those extra-special cakes that require more wow factor. Wrap it tightly in cling film until ready to roll it out or cut it as it dries out when exposed to air.

To **colour** fondant, use the tip of a cocktail stick to add a tiny amount of food colouring paste to fondant and knead it in well. It takes time for the colour to become combined and you can add more as you go, so add slowly and carefully!

To **stick** fondant decorations to a fondant-covered cake, use royal icing, simple syrup, vodka, cooled boiled water or fondant mixed with water. Attach fondant decorations to buttercream at the last minute as moisture in the frosting affects the fondant. For buttercream- or ganache-covered cakes, dampen the area onto which you wish to apply the decoration with a hot metal spatula or spread a little frosting on the back of the fondant before attaching.

Hopefully, your fondant fun will be trouble free, but if you run into any of the following problems, there are solutions. If you find a little tear in your fondant you can usually make good by quickly and firmly rubbing your hands over the surface to bring the edges back together. The heat from your hands makes the sugar more pliable and mends the join. If you accidentally put some food dye on a fondant surface, use a little vodka on a piece of paper towel to rub off the colour. If all else fails, try to alter the design and place a decoration over the imperfection! If you find air bubbles in your fondant, prick them with a clean pin to allow the air to escape. Smooth over the pin-prick mark with your finger. Eliminate air bubbles as they may expand and push out the fondant covering in bulges.

Often, the bottom edge around a fondant-covered cake is a little uneven where it has been cut, so wrap a ribbon or long fondant strip around this edge to conceal the join neatly, giving your cake a much neater finish. Alternatively, pipe a simple border with buttercream or royal icing.

Gumpaste Also known as florist paste, gumpaste is much like fondant but has an added natural ingredient that makes it harden once dry. It is great for making embellishments and fine petals as it can be rolled very thinly, does not tear easily, and dries very quickly. Although technically edible, it has little flavour and is very hard once dry, so is best used for removable decorations that can be kept. Use a little at a time and keep it tightly wrapped in cling film when not working on it, as it dries out much faster than fondant. You can also knead a little gumpaste into fondant if you need a pliable, strong frosting and it will still be pleasant to eat. Gumpaste will keep indefinitely if stored correctly.

Drying and storing fondant/gumpaste decorations Many of the projects in this book use cake decorations made from fondant and/or gumpaste. Making these decorations can be lots of fun! Paper towels, spoons, cocktail sticks and empty egg boxes and apple trays covered in cling film can all be used to help a sugar decoration hold its shape while it dries – just remember to remove any aids used before applying the decorations to cakes.

Air drying sets fondant or gumpaste, allowing it to keep its shape. Allow your decorations to dry overnight at the least. Larger decorations can benefit from one or two days. Humidity can affect drying times, so if it is hot and rainy, your decorations will need at least double the normal drying time. Generally, I leave them out to air dry, but they can be loosely covered with paper towels or stored in a container with air holes or with the lid left ajar. Allow air to circulate around the decoration. Airtight containers will cause the icing to become sticky and soft. If you intend to keep decorations for a while, store them with a sachet of food-grade silica. Fondant and gumpaste decorations do not have an expiration date, strictly speaking, but I would use sugar decorations within a year as they are prone to fading in colour if exposed to light over time.

Any moisture will be absorbed by the sugar in the fondant or gumpaste, causing drooping or 'sweating' (when the surface becomes shiny and sticky, most often from condensation). This is why you should never refrigerate fondant or gumpaste.

decoration know-how

BASIC DECORATION TECHNIQUES

The following techniques will give you a good grounding in the basics of cake decoration.

Piping techniques

Many people find piping intimidating, but it takes only a little practise to create beautiful results. Try piping on wax paper before moving onto cakes and tackling gravity. The key is to maintain a firm, even pressure and be confident in your shaping. Avoid holding the tip too close to the surface and dragging the frosting along – you need to lift the tip a little away from the surface to allow the frosting to drop into place as you guide it along. Use a damp paintbrush to flatten any peaks on freshly piped royal icing.

Layering cakes

Cakes must be completely cool before you start layering. I leave them overnight or for at least a day so they are less likely to crack and fall apart. This is especially important if you are cutting your cakes into shallow layers with lots of filling. I use a cake leveller for this job as it is difficult to achieve flat, even layers if you cut by eye, so using this tool is the key to achieving professional-looking cakes.

1 Set your cake leveller wire to a height that reaches half way up the sides of your cake. Gently hold the cake still with one hand while sawing back and forth with the leveller. Place the top of the cake on the worktop and repeat, cutting off the dome and, thus, creating two even layers.
2 Spread a little buttercream or ganache onto a cake board using an angled metal spatula and place the flat bottom of one layer on top, then press down gently but firmly to fix. (You can do this directly onto a cake stand, but you will not be able to move the cake from the stand. A board is better if covering in fondant or transporting.)
3 With a pastry brush, spread a little Simple Syrup (see page 17) across the top of the cake layer.
4 Spread an even layer of filling on the cake layer and place the other half of the sliced cake on top.
5 Repeat with all the layers, finishing with the flat bottom of one cake on top so that you have a nice even surface.
6 Press down gently to ensure everything levels out and any air is pushed out from between the layers.

TIP: If you are covering your cake in a frosting that is different from the filling (for example, buttercream and jam filling with ganache covering), place some of the ganache in a piping bag, cut a large hole in the tip or attach a large round tip, then pipe a ring around the edge of each layer. Fill inside this ring with the filling. This outer ring, called a dam, stops the filling from oozing out of the sides of the layers, thus avoiding bulges in your finished cake design.

Crumb coating cakes

Once you have layered your cake, give it a crumb coat to trap crumbs within a thin layer of frosting, seal the layers, and provide a foundation for the intended decoration.

1 Using an angled metal spatula, smooth any overspills of frosting on the sides of the cake into all the cracks between the layers.

2 Spoon big dollops of frosting on the top of the cake and start to drag it down the sides with your spatula. Your aim is to smother the sides with frosting, getting into every nook, so don't worry about it looking messy. Add more frosting to the top and cover in the same way as the sides.

3 Take your dough scraper or a large angled metal spatula and slide the edge of the scraper in a smooth continuous motion around the sides of the cake, keeping the scraper or spatula at a right angle to the sides. (A turntable helps with this job.) You are essentially removing most of the excess frosting you initially put on. Remove the excess from your scraper regularly into a separate bowl. Repeat for the top. You are aiming to create a very thin layer of frosting. Leave to rest for 2 hours or refrigerate for 30 minutes.

TIP: If your layers are not stacked straight, you can shift them into line at this stage by pushing with the flat edge of the spatula.

Creating a smooth buttercream or ganache finish

Once your crumb coated cake has rested, repeat the crumb coat process with fresh frosting to achieve a smooth undercoat for rolled fondant or as the final covering.

1 Use the same techniques described above under crumb coating for this job – the key here is to be very generous with your frosting as you need to build up a good coating in order to scrape it off and create clean angles using a dough scraper or angled metal spatula.

2 Once you have applied and smoothed down a first layer, build up more layers. Keep scraping off excess frosting and filling gaps until the sides of the cake are smooth and the line between the board and cake is seamless. Allow to firm up overnight or in the fridge for 30 minutes.

3 Use the hot-knife method for the final smoothing. Place a large angled metal spatula in a jug of just-boiled water for 1 minute. Shake off excess water, then run the spatula around the cake to remove any overhanging frosting and create a perfectly smooth finish. Note that this method can discolour frosting that has been coloured, so either skip this stage or test it on an inconspicuous area first.

TIP: Make sure you use a fresh, crumb-free portion of frosting for this process to give your cake a professional, smooth and elegant finish.

Covering a cake in rolled fondant

Fondant creates a seal around your cake, prolonging freshness by a few days. A fondant covering also makes it possible to add a variety of decorations that won't adhere to a frosting generally, but will adhere to fondant. A fondant-covered cake is also less prone to dents.

Make sure that your cake is as smoothly iced as you can manage and that the frosting has set firm before you cover it with fondant. The smoother the undercoat, the better the fondant result will be. For a 20-cm (8-in) cake, you will usually need about 850 g (1 lb 14 oz) fondant.

Make sure your work surface is clean and dry. Brush your prepared cake with a little Simple Syrup (see page 17). Knead the fondant lightly until it becomes a little more pliable. Dust your work surface with a little icing sugar – you will need to add more as you go to prevent the fondant from sticking, but too much sugar will dry out the icing and cause it to crack. Use a nonstick rolling pin to roll out the fondant.

Once your cake is covered, leave it out to air dry overnight to 'set' it – that is, for it to dry so that it is no longer soft as it was when it was rolled, thus forming a relatively robust casing for the cake. Once covered, the cake inside will be good for three to four days, as the fondant effectively forms a seal and keeps the cake fresh. Avoid using fillings that need refrigerating (such as a cream cheese filling) inside a fondant-covered cake because if you refrigerate a fondant-covered cake the icing will melt.

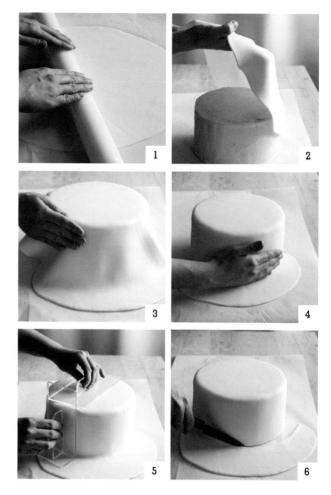

1 Roll out the fondant, rotating and lifting it up occasionally to avoid sticking. Try to maintain a circular shape as this will make it easier to cover the cake. Keep rolling until the fondant is 3 mm (¹/₈ in) thick, ensuring the circle is large enough to cover the entire cake with some extra. Measure the sides and diameter of the top of the cake to check if it helps you roll out the circle to the correct size.
2 Lift up the fondant and place it over the cake, smoothing the top first to squeeze out any air.
3 Next, fix the edges at the top of the cake by lightly running your hands along the fondant.
4 Use your hands to gently fix the sides, with a 'skirt' of fondant left around the bottom.
5 Using fondant smoothers, run along the top and sides of the cake with firm pressure to fix and refine the smoothness of the fondant. For a sharper edge, hold one smoother on the side, with the other placed on top to create a right angle. Now gently move around the cake with the smoothers, defining the top edge as you go.
6 Trim the fondant around the base with a sharp knife or pizza cutter. Be careful not to cut too close as this will expose the under layer.

TIP: To cover a square cake in a layer of fondant, roll out a rough square and fix the edges and corners first before smoothing each side.

Covering a board in rolled fondant

You've spent all this time decorating the cake, so it needs something nice to sit on, right? The key to a professional finish is to place your cake on a larger board that has been covered in fondant of a coordinating colour. Follow the steps below to give your boards a smooth, even covering.

1 Brush the board with a little Simple Syrup (see page 17).
2 Roll out the fondant so that it is large enough to completely cover the board. Lift it up and lower it onto the sticky board.
3 Using smoothers, buff until surface of the fondant is perfectly flat. To do so, apply a light to medium pressure and move the tools in circles so that the fondant surface is flat and smooth.
4 Cut the excess fondant from the edges of the board with a sharp knife.

Allow the fondant to dry and harden for a few days. When you are ready to place your cake on it, apply a few blobs of royal icing to the centre of the board, then position your decorated cake (with its cake board that will be hidden by frosting) on top. Allow to set and your cake will now be secured in place and more stable for transportation. Note that you must have a board beneath your cake if securing your cake on a fondant-covered board, so that it can be moved post-decoration onto the fondant-covered board and to prevent it from melting the fondant on the board due to the moisture within the cake.

TIP: For the perfect finishing touch, wrap a length of 16-mm (⅝-in) ribbon around the edge of the base board and secure it in place with a little non-toxic glue at the back.

Cake transportation

Transporting a cake safely is often the most stressful part of the entire endeavour. A bit of preparation is all it takes to ensure your masterpiece arrives at its destination just as it left the kitchen. The following tips will help.

• If your cake is covered in buttercream or ganache, chill it in the fridge for 30 minutes prior to leaving to firm up the frosting.

• Allow a fondant-covered cake to rest and set overnight in a cool, dry room before transportation.
• Ideally, use a cake box made of thick cardboard that allows airflow to the cake, which will avoid the buildup of condensation that can soften the frosting. Choose a box that is a few centimetres larger than your cake to allow for room around the cake, so decorations are not squashed.
• Use royal icing to fix the cake to a board that is the same size as the box. This will minimise its movement in transit.
• Placing a cake on a flat, level surface is the key to successful cake journeys, so the trunk of a car is a hundred times better than a car seat or lap, both of which will always slope a little.
• Use non-slip matting under the cake box to prevent it from sliding around.
• Remember to always keep the box or cake out of sunlight, which could melt frosting and bleach colour. A sheet or some paper over the box can deflect any stray sunbeams.
• In hot weather, blast the car with air conditioning while in transit and get the cake to a cool, dry place quickly.

Working on a display surface

If you have transported cake layers and are making your cake directly on a cake stand or plate at your venue (or if doing so at home), cut four strips of parchment paper that are each about 10 cm (4 in) wide and 25 cm (10 in) long. Place these on your cake stand or plate in a square shape before you begin layering the cake.

Place the cake on top of the strips so that when you have finished frosting you simply pull the paper away to reveal a clean cake plate.

THE RECIPES

STRAWBERRY DELIGHT

Beautifully pink, dense and moist, this feel-good cake will induce a chorus of 'mmmmm' and 'it's like scones with jam and cream!' The secret ingredient is freeze-dried strawberry powder. This cake is unashamedly feminine, but the boys will be begging for a second slice before they've even finished their first!

strawberry cake

150 g (1¾ oz) unsalted butter, softened
450 g (1 lb) caster sugar
3 eggs
330 g (11½ oz) plain flour
1½ tsp baking powder
½ tsp baking soda
6 tbsp powdered freeze-dried strawberries
1½ tsp vanilla extract
375 ml (13 fl oz) buttermilk
1 quantity Simple Syrup
(see page 17)

strawberry & vanilla frosting

2 tsp vanilla essence
1 batch Italian Meringue Buttercream (see page 14)
1 tbsp strawberry jam
2 tbsp powdered freeze-dried strawberries
Pink food colouring paste

Preheat the oven to 160°C (325°F). Grease and line three 20-cm (8-in) round cake tins.

First make the cake. Using an electric stand mixer set to a high speed, beat the butter and sugar until pale and fluffy. Slowly add the eggs until combined. Reduce the speed to the lowest setting and mix in the flour, baking powder and baking soda. In a bowl, combine the strawberry powder, vanilla extract and buttermilk, then mix this into the batter in the stand mixer bowl. (Add pink food colouring now if you wish to colour the sponge.)

Divide the batter between the prepared cake tins and bake for 30–40 minutes. Allow the cake to cool in the tin for 20 minutes, then transfer to a cooling rack to cool completely. Level the tops with a large serrated knife or cake leveller. Brush each layer with a light covering of simple syrup.

To make the frosting, beat the vanilla into the buttercream, then divide the frosting between two bowls. Flavour one portion with the strawberry jam and freeze-dried strawberry powder (this is for your filling). Set aside the second portion for decorating the cake.

Place one layer onto a cake board or a cake stand. Apply an even layer of the filling across the top to the edges using an angled metal spatula. Repeat with the remaining two layers until the layers are assembled.

Apply a thin crumb coat (see pages 22–23) over the cake with the last of the strawberry buttercream. Chill in the fridge for 30 minutes, then use the ombre piping technique to decorate the cake by following the instructions given on page 30.

OMBRE PIPING TECHNIQUE

1 Divide the vanilla buttercream into three bowls. Tint each portion with the food colouring paste to make three soft shades of pink, graduating gently from deeper pink to a lighter pink. Ensure the graduation between the shades is subtle.

2 Fill three disposable piping bags with the buttercreams in the three shades of pink. Fit a medium round tip onto each bag or snip a 5-mm (¼-in) hole.

3 Starting at the bottom, pipe two dots of the deepest shade vertically to cover a third of the cake's height (you may need more or less dots, depending on the height). Repeat with the mid shade, then with the light shade at the top.

4 Spread each dot from left to right with a metal spatula, leaving a fat curve of frosting at the left. Clean the knife on paper towels between colours. Create a vertical row of dots where the smudge of the last row ends, and repeat until the sides are decorated.

5 Apply the same process to the top of the cake, working in circles. Start with the lightest shade of pink at the edge of the top to blend with the frosting on the sides and fade into the deepest shade in the centre.

6 Ombre piping is a very forgiving cake decorating technique. If you make any mistakes as you work, simply scrape off the frosting and start again in that area until you are satisfied with the result.

CLASSIC NEAPOLITAN

This is such a simple cake, yet there is just something about the colours and flavours that is effortlessly chic and appetising. Keep it understated as I have done here, with the lovely layers on display, or cover the entire cake in frosting for a sweet multilayered surprise.

chocolate fudge cake

3 layers Chocolate Fudge Cake
(see page 11)
1 quantity Simple Syrup
(see page 17), flavoured with vanilla

vanilla, strawberry & chocolate frosting

½ batch Italian Meringue
Buttercream (see page 14) or
Classic Buttercream (see page 14)
2 tbsp strawberry jam + 2 tbsp
freeze-dried strawberry powder
1 tbsp vanilla extract
25 g (1 oz) plain or dark chocolate,
melted and cooled a little

Cut the tops off the cooled cake layers using a serrated knife or a cake leveller. Brush the top of each layer with the vanilla syrup.

To make the frosting, divide the buttercream into three bowls and add one of the flavourings to each bowl, mixing them into the buttercream well.

Place the buttercreams in separate piping bags, each fitted with a large star piping tip (or use the same tip for each frosting, washing it well before switching to the next bag).

Position your first layer onto the cake stand or a cake board and begin piping. For this bottom layer, use the chocolate buttercream. Pipe circles from the outside to the centre of the top of the layer until you have covered the surface with an even amount of frosting.

Carefully position the next cake layer on top, then repeat the piping process with the vanilla frosting.

Now carefully position the top cake layer on top and repeat the process, piping neat rings of strawberry frosting. (For an alternative finish, you might like to leave a small gap around the edge of the top cake layer and roughly pipe over the strawberry frosting, then smooth this layer flat with a small metal spatula. Pipe a neat ring around the top edge.)

Chocolate fudge
& buttercream

SUNSET FADE

Nothing perks up a cake like a little colour. This dreamy, sunset-inspired cake is just the ticket when you're short on time but in need of something uplifting. Try the technique with any cake and change the colours to reflect the flavours.

orange & blueberry cake

535 g (1 lb 3 oz) self-raising flour
450 g (1 lb) caster sugar
4 eggs
1 tsp baking powder
Grated zest of 2 oranges
600 g (1 lb 5 oz) sour cream
Pinch of salt
175 g (6 oz) butter, melted
and cooled
200 g (7 oz) blueberries

frosting & decoration

Grated zest of 2 oranges
2 tbsp Seville orange marmalade
(optional)
1 batch Italian Meringue Buttercream
(see page 14)
Food colouring pastes In lilac,
sunset red and orange
100 g (3½ oz) blueberries, to scatter,
or sprinkles

Preheat the oven to 160°C (325°F). Grease and line three 20-cm (8-in) round cake tins. Place all of the cake ingredients except the butter and blueberries into the large bowl of an electric stand mixer set to a medium speed. Beat to form a smooth dough. Add the melted butter and mix until completely combined. Divide the cake batter equally into the prepared cake tins and scatter a handful of blueberries across the top of each, pressing them into the top a little. Bake for 50–60 minutes.

To make the frosting, beat the orange zest and marmalade into the buttercream. Divide the mixture equally between two bowls (one for filling, one for decorating.)

Place a cooled cake layer onto a cake stand or board and apply an even layer of frosting, then continue layering the cake until it is fully stacked. Apply a thin crumb coat (see pages 22–23) across the top and sides with the last of this buttercream. Chill in the fridge for 30 minutes.

Take the portion of frosting reserved for decorating and divide it equally into three small bowls. Tint each portion using the food colour pastes. Starting with the lilac, use a small angled metal spatula to cover the top of the cake, allowing the frosting to go over the edge to cover the top third of the sides of the cake. Next, apply a horizontal stripe of the sunset red frosting around the middle section of the cake, once again covering approximately one-third of the sides. Now apply the orange frosting in a horizontal stripe around the bottom third of the cake. Make sure the applications are fairly thick and no crumb coating shows through.

Using a clean bench scraper or large angled metal spatula, smooth the frosting around the cake, removing any excess (but ensuring that none of the cake shows through). This will cause the icing shades to blend into each other to create a fading sunset effect. Finish with a scattering of fresh blueberries or sprinkles.

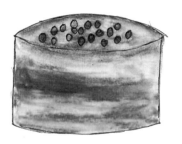

Orange & blueberry

MINI STACKS

Isn't everything cuter in miniature form? Sometimes you want the joy of a layer cake that is easier to share at a party or less intimidating to tackle. These mini stacks are so simple to make – all you need is a batch of cupcakes and some frosting and you're set.

vanilla cupcakes

1 batch Ultimate Sponge Cake batter (see page 11), flavoured with vanilla
1 quantity Simple Syrup (see page 17), flavoured with 1 tsp vanilla extract or the seeds from ½ vanilla pod

frosting

1 batch Classic Buttercream (see page 14), Cream Cheese Frosting (see page 16) or Ganache (see page 15), flavoured/coloured to your taste

TIP: If the cakes seem a little wobbly, insert a skewer, straw or mini cake topper down through the centre of each stack, which will help to hold the little layers together.

Preheat the oven to 160°C (325°F). Line two 12-cup muffin tins with 24 cupcake cases. Spoon the cake batter into the cases until they are each two-thirds full. Bake for approximately 20 minutes until a cocktail stick inserted into the cakes comes out clean. Cool in the muffin tins for 10 minutes, then transfer the cupcakes to a wire rack and leave to cool.

When the cupcakes are completely cool, peel away the cases and slice off the domed tops using a large serrated knife. Next, slice each cupcake in half horizontally. The sponge can be very delicate, so pop them in the freezer for 15 minutes if you have difficulty obtaining a clean cut. (Note that you can use deeper layers if your cupcakes are on the small side and skip cutting them in half, but you will need more cakes to make the correct number of stacks.)

Use a round biscuit cutter that is approximately 5 cm (2 in) in diameter (and, ideally, of the same depth as a cupcake layer) to stamp out a circle from each cake layer, which will give you layers with neat sides, without the conical shape a cupcake often has. Brush each layer with a little syrup.

Place the frosting into a piping bag fitted with a star or plain, large tip. Pipe a circle of frosting onto one cake layer. Carefully position another cake layer on top, then pipe another circle onto that layer. Once again, align another cake layer on top. Now pipe a circle of frosting on top to finish off the mini stacked layer cake. Repeat with the remaining cake layers and frosting to make eight triple-layered stacks.

THE SECRET GARDEN

With all the charm of an English garden in summertime, this fragrant, light cake is scattered with delicate crystalised flowers – the perfect match to the flavours of rose, lime and raspberry. It is easy to crystalise flowers to create effortless-looking decorations. Use edible, pesticide-free flowers, or buy ready made.

rose cake

2 layers Ultimate Sponge Cake
(see page 11), each flavoured with
2 drops rose extract (or to your
taste)
1 quantity Simple Syrup (see page
17), flavoured with 1 drop rose extract

raspberry frosting

½ batch Italian Meringue
Buttercream (see page 14), or Cream
Cheese Frosting (see page 16)
flavoured with 2 tbsp raspberry jam

lime curd

2 eggs
Juice and grated zest of 4 medium
limes
175 g (6 oz) caster sugar
115 g (4 oz) unsalted butter, cut into
cubes and softened

crystalised flowers

25 g (1 oz) pasteurised egg white or
1 egg white, lightly whisked
50 g (1¾ oz) caster sugar
Edible flowers and leaves (try whole
roses or rose petals, violas, pansies,
violets, mimosa, cowslips, sweet
geranium leaves, carnations, mint
leaves, lavender and primroses)

First make the curd. Whisk the eggs in a medium-sized saucepan, then add the remaining ingredients. Set the saucepan over a medium heat. Whisk continuously for about 8 minutes until the mixture thickens. Reduce the heat to low and allow the curd to simmer gently for another minute, continuing to whisk. Remove the saucepan off the heat and allow the curd to cool to room temperature, then chill in the fridge until it has a spreadable consistency. (If you are making the curd ahead of time, store it in a sterilised jar in the fridge for two to three weeks.)

To make the crystalised flowers, line a large baking tray with wax paper. Place the egg white in a small bowl and the sugar in another. Hold the flower or leaf and paint it with egg white, ensuring even coverage. Use a medium-sized (food-only) paintbrush for this job. Sprinkle over the sugar, making sure all the egg white is covered, then shake off the excess. Lay the flowers or leaves on the lined baking tray and leave to set in a dry, warm place overnight. Store in an airtight container lined with wax paper. They are very fragile, so stack them only a couple of layers deep.

To assemble the cake, level the tops of the two cooled sponge cakes using a serrated knife or cake leveller. Now cut each of the two cake layers in half horizontally to create four layers. Brush the sponges with syrup and layer alternately with lime curd and raspberry frosting – you should have two layers of curd and one of frosting. Crumb coat (see pages 22–23) with frosting, chill for 30 minutes, and finish with a smoother covering of raspberry frosting.

Attach the flowers while the frosting is still soft to make sure they stick. Pile up the crystalised flowers on top, saving a handful. Press these into the sides to give the impression of the flowers tumbling down.

ROSETTE SWIRLS

Piped rosette swirls lend a beautiful texture to the finish of this cake. A steady hand, a little time and a piping bag is all you need for the decoration technique. If you make a mistake, simply scrape it off and start again. Lime and blackberry is a match made in heaven, and the soft purple shade that comes from the blackberries really enhances the look of the piping.

lime cake

3 batches Ultimate Sponge Cake batter (see page 11), each flavoured with the zest and juice of 1 lime
1 quantity Simple Syrup (see page 17), flavoured with the grated zest and juice of 1 lime

blackberry frosting & decoration

100 g (3½ oz) fresh blackberries
25 g (1 oz) caster sugar
1 batch of Italian Meringue Buttercream (see page 14)
Approximately 50 g (1¾ oz) berries or cherries, to decorate

Blackberry & lime

Preheat the oven to 160°C (325°F). Grease and line three 20-cm (8-in) round cake tins. Divide the cake mixture equally between the prepared tins and bake for 40–45 minutes until a cocktail stick inserted into the centre comes out clean. Allow to cool in the tins for 20 minutes, then turn out onto a wire rack and allow to cool completely.

Make a blackberry paste to flavour and colour the frosting. Place the blackberries in a blender and pulse until smooth. Pour them into a sieve placed over a bowl to remove the seeds. Mix the sugar into the sieved paste. Now beat the blackberry paste into the buttercream 1 tbsp at a time until you achieve a nice pale purple colour and the buttercream is flavoured to your taste. Divide the buttercream equally between two bowls (one for filling, the other for piping).

Level the cake tops with a large serrated knife or cake leveller. Brush each cake layer with a light covering of lime-flavoured syrup. Place your first layer onto a cake stand or 20-cm (8-in) round cake board. Apply an even layer of blackberry buttercream and continue layering until the cake is fully stacked. Apply a thin crumb coat (see pages 22–23) across the top and sides. Chill in the fridge for 30 minutes.

Fit a medium star tip on your piping bag and fill the bag with the remaining blackberry buttercream. Before you begin to decorate your cake, practise piping rosettes on a sheet of wax paper. Start piping each rosette in the centre, swirling the buttercream round in a spiral before finishing with decreasing pressure, which will blend the end of the piping into the side of the rosette. Your next rosette will cover the end of the previous one.

Starting at the bottom of the cake, pipe columns of rosettes until the sides are covered. Pipe the same number of rosettes in each column and make sure they appear side by side on the horizontal rows for a neat finish. Use a stainless steel ruler to mark the position of each rosette on the crumb coat if you need help in achieving straight columns. Repeat the rosettes on the top of the cake, starting from the centre and working outwards in circles.

Place a berry or cherry onto the centre of each rosette on the top of the cake to finish.

LEMON CLOUD CAKE

This is a classic idea re-created in layer cake form. A lemony tang runs through this meringue-covered cake. If you have a blowtorch, toasting the fluffy frosting will add another layer of flavour and emphasise the gorgeous texture.

lemon cake

2 layers Ultimate Sponge Cake (see page 11), each flavoured with the grated zest and juice of 1 lemon
1 quantity Simple Syrup (see page 17), flavoured with the grated zest and juice of 1 lemon

lemon curd

4 large eggs
Juice and grated zest of 4 large lemons
350 g (12 oz) caster sugar
225 g (8 oz) unsalted butter, cubed and softened

meringue frosting

85 g (3 oz) pasteurised egg whites or 2 extra large egg whites
225 g (8 oz) caster sugar
5 tbsp water
Pinch of cream of tartar

Lemon & meringue

Make the lemon curd ahead of time. Whisk the eggs in a medium-sized saucepan, then add the remaining ingredients and set the saucepan over a medium heat. Whisk continuously for about 8 minutes until the mixture thickens. Reduce the heat to low and let the curd gently simmer for another minute, continuing to whisk. Allow to cool to room temperature, then chill in the fridge until the curd has a spreadable consistency.

Level the tops of the two cooled cakes and cut each cake in half horizontally using a large serrated knife or cake leveller to create four layers. Brush the sponges with lemon-flavoured syrup. Place your first layer onto a cake stand or 20-cm (8-in) round cake board and apply an even layer of lemon curd. Continue layering in this way until the cake is fully stacked.

Now make the meringue frosting. Put all of the ingredients into a heatproof bowl and set this over a saucepan of simmering water. Make sure that the bottom of the bowl doesn't touch the water beneath it. Using a handheld blender, whip the mixture in the bowl for 7 minutes until stiff peaks form. Remove the bowl from the saucepan as soon as the mixture is glossy and holds its peaks. The meringue will start to set a little once whipped, so it needs to be used right away.

As soon as the meringue is made, apply a thin layer all over the sides and top of the cake using a large angled metal spatula. Add another thick layer of meringue until the cake is covered, then swirl, twist, and flick using the spatula to create a lovely billowy texture.

Now, using a chef's blowtorch, carefully work your way around the cake, toasting the meringue in places until golden. This step isn't essential, so you can leave the frosting white and fluffy if you prefer, but toasting sections of it does emphasise the texture and gives the cake a delicious toasted flavour note.

RED RASPBERRY VELVET

Nothing beats a fruit-topped cake gleaming with glaze, and this one combines classic continental style with eye-catching red velvet cake – an American classic. Discs of marzipan wrapped around the sides is a neat and classy way of decorating, but you can use modelling chocolate or fondant if you prefer.

red velvet cake

3 layers Red Velvet Cake
(see page 12)
1 quantity Simple Syrup (see page 17)
flavoured with 1 tsp vanilla extract or
the seeds from ½ vanilla pod

vanilla frosting

1 batch Cream Cheese Frosting
(see page 16), flavoured with 2 tsp
vanilla extract or the seeds from
1 vanilla pod

marzipan decoration

Icing sugar, for dusting
250 g (9 oz) natural marzipan
150 g (5½ oz) fresh raspberries
50 g (1¾ oz) seedless raspberry jam

Red velvet with marzipan

Level the tops of the three layers of Red Velvet Cake using a large serrated knife or a cake leveller. Using a pastry brush, brush the sponges with simple syrup.

Place the first layer on a cake stand or cake board. Now stack the layers using half of the frosting, spreading an equal amount of frosting between each layer with an angled metal spatula. Crumb coat the cake and finish with the remaining frosting (see pages 22–23).

To make the marzipan decorations, dust your work surface with a little icing sugar. Using a nonstick rolling pin, roll out the marzipan to a thickness of approximately 3 mm (⅛ in). Taking a round pastry cutter with a diameter that is approximately equal to the height of the cake or a little less, cut out enough discs to wrap around the sides of the cake, bearing in mind that you will be overlapping them.

While the frosting is still tacky, take a disc of marzipan and gently press it onto the side of the cake to fix it in place. Position the next disc so that it overlaps the previous one by about half and press this into place to fix it. Continue in this way all around the cake until the sides are decorated by a ring of overlapping marzipan discs.

Pile the fresh raspberries on top of the cake. Warm the raspberry jam in a saucepan until it is loose but not hot. Brush the raspberries with plenty of jam until they are coated and glossy.

Wrap approximately 1 m (1 yd) of ribbon around the middle of the cake and fix it in place by tying a bow.

MACARON MAGIC

Not only do French macarons give this cake a fabulous pop of stylish colour,
they also provide a lovely chewy texture to contrast with the soft sponge.
Macarons are not really as difficult to make as their reputation would have you
think. A little patience and practise will yield fantastic results. Of course, if time
is not on your side, simply buy some from a patisserie.

prepared cake

1 x 20-cm (8-in) layered cake, filled,
crumb coated and covered
in a smooth layer of buttercream
frosting (see pages 10–25 for
guidance)

macarons

125 g (4½ oz) icing sugar
140 g (5 oz) ground almonds
130 g (4½ oz) pasteurised egg whites
or 4 large egg whites
Pinch of salt
100 g (3½ oz) caster sugar
Food colouring paste

ganache

½ batch dark chocolate Ganache
(see page 15)

*Orange frosting with
a ganache drizzle*

Prepare the macarons the day before you need them. Preheat the oven
to 160°C (320°F). Blend the icing sugar and almonds in a food processor
to a very fine mixture, then sieve the mixture into a bowl to remove any
large pieces. Reserve 2 tbsp of egg whites and put the remainder into a
bowl. Whisk the egg whites with the salt until foamy, then gradually whisk
in the caster sugar until the mixture is thick and glossy. Add the food
colouring paste and whip through until you have your desired colour.
Fold in half the almond mixture and mix well, using a spatula to cut and
fold the mixture. Mix in the remaining half. Whisk the reserved egg
whites in a bowl until frothy and add to the mixture, folding them in
gently to loosen the batter until it is shiny and has a thick, ribbon-like
consistency as it falls from the spatula. Spoon the mixture into a piping
bag fitted with a medium round tip or snip a 5-mm (¼-in) hole across
the tip.

Line 2 baking sheets with parchment paper. Pipe small rounds of the
macaron mixture onto the baking sheets – they should have a diameter
of approximately 3 cm (1¼ in). Give the baking sheets a sharp tap
on the work surface to remove air bubbles. Leave to stand at room
temperature for 30 minutes to allow each of the piped rounds to form a
slight skin. This is important and will ensure a good 'foot' (the ruffle that
forms on the bottom edges, which will show that the macarons have
risen and cooked properly). Bake for 15 minutes. Remove from the oven
and leave to cool on the baking sheet.

Place half of the ganache into a piping bag and snip a 5-mm (¼-in) hole
across the tip. Pipe even blobs of ganache onto the flat side of half of the
macaron shells and sandwich together with the remaining shells. Place
the filled macarons in an airtight container and refrigerate overnight to

allow the texture to develop. (Note that this recipe yields more macaron shells than needed. Wrap unfilled shells in cling film and freeze for up to one month. Defrost to room temperature before use.)

To decorate the cake, gently warm the remaining ganache and spread it over the top of the prepared frosted cake with a spatula. Work quickly and gently, and nudge the ganache at the edges of the cake to encourage it to drip down the sides. Remember that

the ganache will continue to run down the sides, so don't overdo it – you want the drips to go about half-way down the sides of the cake.

If you have any coloured buttercream left over from your cake covering, place it in a piping bag fitted with a large star or plain tip. If you don't have any left, use the remaining ganache. Pipe swirls around the top edge of the cake, then gently push one macaron, on its side, into each swirl.

MERINGUE STACK

While this stack of meringues with berries and cream could be considered more of a dessert than a cake, I couldn't resist sharing it for its lightness and rustic charm. It is gluten free, so is ideal to make for anyone with a wheat intolerance.

pistachio meringue

165 g (5¾ oz) pasteurised egg whites or 5 egg whites
275 g (9¾ oz) caster sugar
Green food colouring paste (optional)
200 g (7 oz) coarsely ground pistachio nuts

mascarpone frosting

240 ml (8 fl oz) double cream plus 1–2 tbsp more
25 g (1 oz) caster sugar
500 g (1 lb 2 oz) mascarpone
1 tsp vanilla extract
1 tbsp finely chopped fresh mint (optional)

filling & decoration

400 g (14 oz) mixed fresh berries, including raspberries, strawberries, blueberries and blackberries
50 g (1¾ oz) white chocolate, melted

Pistachio & mascarpone layers

To make the meringue layers, preheat the oven to 140°C (275°F). Trace around a 20-cm (8-in) round cake tin onto a sheet of parchment paper four times and place each of these templates onto a baking tray (or place two on a sheet, if your baking trays are large enough).

Whisk the egg whites in a very clean bowl until foamy. Now gradually sprinkle in the sugar while whisking until the mixture is smooth and glossy and firm peaks form. Fold in the food colouring, if using, and the pistachio nuts. Put the mixture into a piping bag fitted with a large, plain tip and fill in each of the circle templates by piping in concentric circles, keeping 1 cm (½ in) inside the edges to allow for expansion.

Bake for approximately 90 minutes, rotating the sheets between shelves once or twice to ensure even colouring. After 60 minutes, turn off the oven and leave the meringue layers inside for 30 minutes, then remove from the oven and cool to room temperature.

For the mascarpone frosting, place the cream and sugar into a large mixing bowl and whisk until firm. Fold through the mascarpone carefully until well combined. Add the vanilla and fresh mint, if using, and stir through until they are evenly distributed. Add a little more cream to loosen the mixture if needed.

Now assemble the stack. Place the first layer onto a cake stand or cake board. Spread a quarter of the frosting evenly over it using an angled metal spatula. Scatter a handful of berries across the frosting and gently press them in. Repeat with the remaining layers.

For the top, pile the berries onto the final layer of frosting so that they are higher in the middle. Drizzle with melted white chocolate to finish.

LIQUID GOLD

I know I'm not meant to have favourites, but this banana cake combines the most irresistible flavours that make it the kind of cake you daydream about. It's bold, simple in decoration, but so inviting and perfect for sharing over coffee.

banana choc chip cake

240 g (8½ oz) unsalted butter, softened
400 g (14 oz) caster sugar
4 eggs
4 very ripe medium or large bananas, broken into chunks
225 g (8 oz) sour cream
1 tbsp vanilla extract
400 g (14 oz) plain flour
2 tsp baking soda
200 g (7 oz) dark chocolate chips or chunks (minimum 53 per cent cocoa solids)

salted caramel sauce

225 g (8 oz) caster sugar
85 g (3 oz) unsalted butter, chopped into chunks
125 ml (4 fl oz) double cream
60 ml (2 fl oz) water
½ tsp flaked sea salt

peanut butter frosting

½ batch Italian Meringue Buttercream (see page 14) flavoured with 2 tbsp peanut butter

peanut praline

150 g (5½ oz) caster sugar
2 tbsp water
100 g (3½ oz) salted peanuts

First, make the cake. Preheat the oven to 160°C (325°F). Grease and line two 20-cm (8-in) round cake tins. Beat the butter and sugar until pale and fluffy using an electric stand mixer set to a high speed. Gradually add the eggs until combined. Gradually add the banana chunks until combined. Beat in the sour cream and vanilla. Gently mix in the flour and baking soda, then stir in the chocolate chips by hand. Divide the mixture equally between the prepared tins and bake for approximately 50–60 minutes.

To make the salted caramel, heat the sugar and water in a large saucepan set over a medium-high heat. Do not stir the sugar, but swirl the saucepan to help it dissolve if necessary. When the liquid sugar becomes deep amber, add the butter. The mixture will foam up and thicken. Whisk until the butter melts, then take the saucepan off the heat. Add the cream (the mixture will foam up again) and continue to whisk to incorporate. Add the salt and whisk until the sauce is smooth. Cool in the saucepan to room temperature. Don't worry if the sauce seems a bit too thin at first – it will thicken as it cools. Store in the fridge for up to two weeks.

Level the tops of the cakes and cut them in half to create four layers. Place the first layer on a cake stand or cake board. Apply a layer of buttercream, followed with a drizzle of caramel sauce. Try to get some sauce to drip off the edges and down the sides, but bear in mind that too much sauce will make the layers unsteady. Continue layering in this way until the cake is fully stacked. Spread an even and neat layer of buttercream on the top.

For the praline, heat the sugar and water in a large saucepan set over a medium-high heat until the sugar is dissolved. Do not stir. Scatter the peanuts across a baking sheet lined with parchment paper. When the liquid sugar is a deep amber colour, pour it over the nuts. Spread it with an oiled spatula to create an even, thin layer. Be careful – it will be very hot. Allow to set, then tap the praline with the end of a rolling pin to break the sheet into shards. Stick these into the top of the cake at angles.

TRUFFLE DECADENCE

Such decadence! This cake is a chocolate lover's dream. Studded with melt-in-the-mouth truffles, it is most definitely a case of style as well as substance. Hand-rolled truffles are super easy to make, but be prepared to get messy. Shop-bought chocolates will work, too.

prepared cake

1 x 20-cm (8-in) layered cake, filled, crumb coated and covered in a smooth layer of buttercream or ganache (see pages 10-25 for guidance)

chocolate truffles

1½ batches dark chocolate Ganache (see page 15)
Approximately 200 g (7 oz) cocoa powder, for rolling

TIPS: The heat from your hands will melt the ganache, so you will get messy. If your hands become too sticky during the truffle rolling, wash them frequently to ensure a neat finish. Try rolling a few truffles in gold lustre for a luxe finish, or make white chocolate truffles and roll them in shredded coconut.

To make the truffles, prepare the ganache and allow it to set until it is firm but still malleable. You can pop the bowl in the fridge to speed up the setting process, but remember to stir it every 10 minutes to prevent the mixture from hardening. Place roughly 100 g (3½ oz) of the ganache into a small bowl and set to one side.

Sprinkle the cocoa powder over a large plate or tray. Take 1 tbsp of ganache and roll it quickly in the palms of your hands to make a ball. Now push the ball around in the cocoa powder until it has an even coating. Continue making truffles in this way, placing the dusted truffles on a clean plate or tray as you go. Put them in the fridge for 30–60 minutes to allow them to firm up. Then, using a sharp knife, cut the truffles in half.

Put the ganache you set aside into a piping bag fitted with a medium plain tip or snip a 5-mm (¼-in) hole across the tip. Pipe a little blob of soft ganache onto the side of the cake at the bottom edge, then press the cut side of a truffle onto it. Continue applying the truffles to the cake in this way, working around the bottom edge, then moving upwards row by row.

Dust the top of the cake with cocoa powder to finish.

buried treasure

RAINBOW SURPRISE

Is there anything more appealing than a myriad of bright colours? These vibrant layers scream 'let's celebrate!' The soft buttercream frosting hints at a surprise that children and adults alike will enjoy. This is a deceptively easy cake to create – simply set aside the time to tint and bake the layers.

rainbow cake

2 batches Ultimate Sponge
Cake batter (see page 11), each
flavoured with 1 tsp vanilla extract
6 food colouring pastes
1 quantity Simple Syrup
(see page 17), flavoured with ¼ tsp
vanilla extract

buttercream frosting

1 batch Italian Meringue
Buttercream (see page 14),
flavoured to complement the
vanilla sponge cake

Preheat the oven to 160°C (350°F). Grease and line three 15-cm (6-in) round cake tins. You'll re-use the tins until six layers are baked, relining each time (work quickly so the remaining cake batter doesn't lose its lift.)

Divide the cake batter into six small bowls. You can weigh the mixing bowl before you make the batter, then weigh the batter in the bowl once mixed and subtract the bowl weight. Divide the total weight of the cake batter by 6 and weigh out these portions into the six small bowls.

Starting with a little paste, gently but thoroughly mix one colour into each portion of batter until you have a rainbow of six vibrant colours. Pour one portion of batter into each of the three prepared tins and bake for 25–30 minutes until the sponge is springy and a cocktail stick inserted into the centre comes out clean. Allow the cakes to cool in the tins for 5 minutes, then turn out onto a wire rack. Reline and grease the tins and bake the final three layers. Allow the cake layers to cool completely.

Once cool, cut off any domed tops with a large serrated knife or cake leveller. Brush each layer with a light covering of simple syrup. Place the first sponge cake layer on a cake board, a cake stand or plate and, using a medium or large angled metal spatula, spread an even layer of buttercream over the top surface up to the edges. Position another sponge cake layer on top and repeat this process until all the layers are stacked. Put 50 g (1¾ oz) of the remaining buttercream into a small bowl and set to one side.

Crumb coat your assembled cake (see pages 22–23) by applying a thin layer of buttercream with an angled spatula until all gaps are filled. Chill in the fridge for 30 minutes. Now apply the final, thicker layer of buttercream (see page 23 for frosting tips). Use a dough scraper or angled spatula to smooth and work the buttercream, then finish with the hot-knife method (see page 23).

Divide the remaining frosting into 6 portions and colour each in one of the six shades you used for the cake layers. Using a piping bag fitted with a small, plain tip, pipe dots randomly over the cake, or place dots of each colour on the outside of the cake to reflect where those colours appear on the inside of the cake, which looks striking once the cake is cut.

NATURAL DYES

You can make your own natural food dyes (see below for suggestions), but for traditional colours in strong, vibrant shades, artificial food colours are probably your best bet. Alternatively, you can purchase vegetable-based natural food dyes, although they are more expensive than the traditional synthetic versions.

RED Juice beetroot in a juicer or use the liquid from tinned beetroot.

ORANGE Juice carrots in a juicer or buy carrot juice.

YELLOW Try using turmeric powder or an egg yolk.

GREEN Juice spinach in a juicer.

BLUE Microwave roughly 40 g (1½ oz) frozen blueberries in 30-second intervals until they start to burst. Sieve before use.

PURPLE Microwave roughly 40 g (1½ oz) frozen blackberries in 30-second intervals until they start to burst. Strain before use.

CAMOUFLAGE

So often, cake can be a little, well, girly. It's just too easy to make pretty frosting and flowers. A camouflage-patterned interior makes this the perfect man cake, but switch the green to pink and you have a cute girly version. This is essentially a classic marble cake, so choose any colour combination you like.

mint & chocolate cake

3 batches Ultimate Sponge Cake batter (see page 11), each flavoured with 2 drops peppermint extract
1 tbsp cocoa powder
25 g (1 oz) plain or dark chocolate, melted
Khaki green food colouring paste
1 quantity Simple Syrup
(see page 17), flavoured with 1 drop peppermint extract

mint & chocolate frosting

1 batch dark chocolate Ganache (see page 15)
130 g (4¾ oz) unsalted butter, softened
4 drops peppermint extract
½ batch Italian Meringue Buttercream (see page 14) or Classic Buttercream (see page 14), flavoured with 2 drops peppermint extract

Chocolate & mint marble cake

Preheat the oven to 160°C (325°F). Grease and line three 20-cm (8-in) round cake tins. Divide the cake batter into three equal portions, leaving one portion in the electric stand mixer bowl. Stir the cocoa powder and melted chocolate into the portion in the stand mixer with the mixer set to a slow speed, and colour the other portion khaki green. You should now have three colours – original beige, chocolate brown and khaki green. Using a large spoon, drop alternating colours of batter randomly into your three cake tins until they all contain a roughly equal amount of batter in each. Bake for 45–50 minutes and allow to cool.

Using a large serrated knife or cake leveller, cut off the domed tops of the cake layers.

Whip the ganache with the butter and peppermint for a minute until lightened, but be careful not to over-whip, otherwise the mixture will separate. (It's also crucial that the ganache is at room temperature when you start, and is not too firm nor too thin.) Fill a piping bag with roughly half the ganache and cut a hole into the tip with a diameter of approximately 1 cm (½ in).

Place the first layer on a cake stand or board and brush it with an even amount of the syrup. Pipe a border around the edge of the top of the layer and fill the space inside this dam with an even layer of the peppermint buttercream. Align the next layer and repeat the process until the cake is fully stacked.

If you have any ganache left in the piping bag, squeeze it onto the cake and crumb coat, using extra ganache if necessary. Chill the cake in the fridge for 30 minutes. Apply the final, thicker layer of ganache and smooth it with a bench scraper or large angled metal spatula.

While the ganache is still soft, take a small angled metal spatula and swipe the frosting from the bottom upwards, creating an indented stripe. Continue all the way around the sides of the cake. Now repeat the motion in circles on the top of the cake, starting from the outer edge and working your way in toward the centre of the cake. If you find that the ganache is firming up, try dipping your palette knife in hot water to warm the metal, which should make it easier to move it through the ganache.

CUBIST COOL

This chocolate, coffee and salted honey cake tastes as good as it looks. Choose a stylish colour scheme of four colours for the outside decoration. The inside has a chic chess board design in muted tones to offset the bright exterior.

coffee cake

2 layers Ultimate Sponge Cake (see page 11), each flavoured with 2 tsp espresso or coffee powder, made in 20-cm (8-in) square cake tins

chocolate cake

200 ml (7 fl oz) whole milk
150 g (5½ oz) dark or plain chocolate chips (minimum 53 per cent cocoa solids) or, if using a block, chopped finely
2 tsp espresso or coffee powder (optional)
2 tsp vanilla extract
450 g (1 lb) dark or light brown sugar
150 g (5½ oz) unsalted butter, softened
4 eggs
300 g (10½ oz) plain flour
3 tbsp cocoa powder
1 tsp baking powder
1 tsp baking soda

frosting & decoration

1 batch Italian Meringue Buttercream (see page 14), flavoured with 2 tbsp honey and ¼ tsp salt
¾ batch dark chocolate Ganache (see page 15)
1.8 kg (4 lb) ready-to-use white fondant
4 food colouring pastes
Icing sugar, for dusting
Small amount of Simple Syrup (see page 17) or edible glue

Preheat the oven to 160°C (325°F). Grease and line two 20-cm (8-in) square cake tins.

While the two coffee sponge cakes are cooling, make the chocolate sponge cakes. Place the milk, chocolate, coffee, vanilla and half the brown sugar in a medium-sized saucepan set over a medium-low heat, stirring occasionally. Take the saucepan off the heat once the chocolate has melted.

In the large bowl of an electric stand mixer set to a high speed, beat together the butter and remaining sugar until pale and fluffy. Gradually add the eggs until combined.

In a separate bowl, sieve together the flour, cocoa powder, baking powder and baking soda, then add the mixture to the contents of the stand mixer bowl and beat until combined. Reduce the speed setting to low and, while the chocolate mixture is still hot, carefully pour it into the cake batter and incorporate it into the mixture.

Divide the cake batter between the two prepared cake tins and bake for 45–50 minutes. Cover the tins with aluminium foil for the final 10–15 minutes to prevent the cakes becoming too dark. Leave to cool.

Once all the cake layers are completely cool, level the tops with a large serrated knife or cake leveller so that they are all of the same height. Stack the cakes on a tray with a sheet of parchment paper between each layer and refrigerate for 1 hour or place in the freezer for 30 minutes to firm up the sponge cakes, which makes it easier to carve them.

Now it's time for the fun! To create the chess board pattern inside the cake, you need to cut hollow squares out of each of your sponge cakes according to the pattern shown on the template (see page 157). Lift one

cake layer on a sheet of parchment paper onto your work surface. Starting from the outside edge, cut a hollow square 2.5 cm (1 in) in from the sides of the cake. Carefully lift away the outer hollow square and repeat the process until you reach the central square, which will measure 5 x 5 cm (2 x 2 in). Repeat this cutting process with all the cake layers.

Once you have cut all the hollow squares, use an angled metal spatula to apply 5 mm (¼ in) of buttercream to the internal edges of each square. This will act as a glue to hold the hollow squares together when you rebuild each cake layer using hollow squares of alternating colours. Start with a chocolate-flavoured exterior hollow square. Place the coffee-flavoured hollow square that is the next size down inside it. Now place the correct-sized chocolate-flavoured hollow square inside that one, and finish with one of the squares of coffee-flavoured sponge cake. Repeat this configuration once more, then swap over with the remaining squares to begin each layer with a coffee-flavoured exterior hollow square.

Smear a little buttercream onto your cake stand or board and carefully place the first layer (choose one with a chocolate-flavoured external square) on top firmly. Smooth an even layer of buttercream over the cake layer, then align the next layer (which should have a coffee-flavoured external square) on top. Repeat with the remaining two layers. Apply a crumb coat (see pages 22–23) with ganache to the top and sides of the assembled cake, then leave it to rest for 30 minutes. Apply a second layer of ganache, using a bench scraper and the hot-knife method (see page 23) to create a smooth finish with sharp edges.

To decorate the cake, roll out 1 kg (2 lb 4 oz) of the fondant to a thickness of 3 mm (⅛ in) and use it to cover the cake (see page 24). Divide the remaining fondant into four equal chunks (if you are using four colours). Tint each portion using a food colouring

paste until you achieve the shade you want. Keep the portions of fondant you're not working with wrapped up tightly in cling film to stop them from drying out.

Using a nonstick rolling pin, roll out your first fondant portion to a thickness of approximately 3 mm (⅛ in). Using a square cutter measuring 2.5 x 2.5 cm (1 x 1 in), or measuring accurately with a steel ruler and cutting with a sharp knife, cut out fondant squares. Repeat with all the colours and set them aside on a flat, clean surface as you work. Let the fondant squares dry for a couple of hours, which makes them easier to handle when you move them.

Attach the squares to the sides of the cake using a little syrup or edible glue. Paint the syrup or glue onto the back of each square. Start around the bottom of the sides of the cake and work your way up, then work around the outside edges of the top towards the centre. You could measure the sides first to devise an accurate placement plan, or simply wing it – if you work at a good pace there is always time to slide the squares around a little before the syrup sets.

Chocolate & coffee
chess board cake

GROOVY BABY

You can choose your favourite colours for these psychedelic beauties, which are very cute in miniature form. Or you could re-create them on a larger scale – simply apply the same technique to larger cake tins with more cake batter according to the cake-scaling guide on page 10.

tie-dye vanilla cake

1 batch Ultimate Sponge Cake batter (see page 11), flavoured with 1 tsp vanilla extract
Food colouring pastes
½ quantity Simple Syrup (see page 17), flavoured with 1 tsp vanilla extract

frosting & fondant

1 batch Classic Buttercream (see page 14), flavoured with 2 tsp vanilla extract
1 kg (2 lb 4 oz) ready-to-use white fondant
Food colouring pastes
Icing sugar, for dusting

Preheat the oven to 160°C (325°F). Grease and line a 20-cm (8-in) square cake tin. Divide the cake batter into three to four small bowls and add a different food colour to each bowl, mixing in a little at a time until incorporated.

Spoon alternating colours of batter into the prepared tin until all the batter is used. Swirl a knife or skewer through the batter to marble the colours, but don't overwork – make sure you retain definition between the colours. Bake for 45–50 minutes.

Level the top of the cake with a large serrated knife or cake leveller. Cut it in half horizontally to create two layers. Using a round pastry cutter that is approximately 6 cm (2½ in) in diameter, cut out eighteen sponge circles from the two layers of sponge. It will be quite a tight fit, so plan your cutting and position your cutter thoughtfully.

Use a small palette knife to smear a little buttercream onto nine cake card bases with a diameter of 6 cm (2½ in), then press a sponge circle onto each card. Brush these bottom layers with a little syrup, then spread an even amount of buttercream over the top of each bottom layer. Press the next layer on top and brush with a little syrup.

Using the remaining buttercream, crumb coat each mini cake (see pages 22–23). Try to achieve as smooth a finish as you can – it can be tricky with mini cakes. Chill in the fridge for 15 minutes.

Divide the white fondant into two equal portions. Wrap one portion tightly in cling film and put it to one side. Split the remaining portion into three to four chunks and knead a small amount of food colouring paste into each one. Now knead the plain fondant with the coloured fondants

Mini tie-dye vanilla sponges

until just marbled. Do not overmix or the colours will become muddy. Also, when you roll out the fondant, the marble effect will continue to develop so it is better to under-mix at this stage.

Take a quarter of this marbled fondant and wrap up the rest tightly in cling film and set to one side. Dust your work surface with icing sugar. Using a nonstick rolling pin, roll out the portion of fondant to a thickness of about 3 mm (¹/₈ in). Cut a square of fondant that is large enough to cover one of the cakes, lift it over a cake, and smooth down the sides (see page 24 for tips on covering a cake with fondant).

Trim off the excess around the bottom edge with a sharp knife. Polish and smooth the sides with fondant smoothers. Repeat the process for each cake one at a time. If it takes you some time to cover each cake, don't leave the rolled-out fondant to dry. Instead, take a small amount of fondant and roll it out for each cake as you go.

MODERN ART SHAPES

The beauty of this cake is that you don't have to be too precise to get amazing results. Also, it will turn out differently every time. The dark chocolate cake provides the perfect background for bright pops of colour, with every slice containing its own unique combination of abstract shapes.

coloured cake shapes

150 g (5½ oz) unsalted butter, cubed
135 ml (4½ fl oz) water
150 g (5½ oz) white chocolate chips, or if using a block, chopped finely
150 g (5½ oz) plain flour
150 g (5½ oz) self-raising flour
200 g (7 oz) caster sugar
Pinch of salt
2 eggs, lightly beaten
1 tsp vanilla extract
Food colouring pastes in bold colours, such as orange, yellow and blue

chocolate fudge cake

3 batches Chocolate Fudge Cake batter (see page 11)

ganache frosting

1 batch Ganache (see page 15)
150 g (5½ oz) unsalted butter, softened

chocolate shards

200 g (7 oz) plain or dark chocolate chips (minimum 53 per cent cocoa solids) or, if using a block, chopped finely

First, make the coloured shapes. Preheat the oven to 160°C (325°F). Line two 12-cup muffin tins with 24 cupcake cases.

In a small saucepan, gently melt the butter into the water, stirring. Take the saucepan off the heat and stir in the white chocolate until it has melted and combined with the butter and water mixture.

Sieve the flours into a bowl and add the sugar and salt. Pour the white chocolate mixture, eggs and vanilla into the bowl and beat until combined. Divide the batter into at least three bowls and colour each portion using a food colouring paste. Spoon the mixtures into the cupcake cases so they are approximately two-thirds full and bake for 20 minutes. Transfer to a wire rack and leave to cool.

Make the cake. Preheat the oven to 160°C (325°F). Grease and line three 20-cm (8-in) round cake tins. Peel away the paper cases from the cupcakes and cut them into squares, triangles and circles with a sharp knife. Make the shapes 2.5–5 cm (1–2 in) in size. Spread just enough chocolate cake batter into the cake tins to cover the bottoms. Scatter the shapes around the tins, ensuring they are evenly distributed. Pour the remaining batter over the shapes, dividing it equally among the tins. Bake for 60–70 minutes. Cool the cakes in the tins for 20 minutes, then turn out onto a wire rack and cool completely.

While the cakes are baking, make the chocolate shards using the double-boiler method. Place the chocolate in a heatproof bowl set over a saucepan of simmering water, ensuring the bottom of the bowl does not touch the water. Gently stir until the chocolate is just melted and remove the bowl from the saucepan.

Place a large piece of wax paper onto a baking tray. Pour the warm chocolate onto the paper and spread with an angled metal spatula until the paper is covered in a thin, even layer. Place another piece of wax paper on top of the chocolate, pressing down to remove air bubbles. Refrigerate for at least 2 hours to harden. Peel back the top layer of paper and score lines on the chocolate surface with a sharp knife to encourage the chocolate to break into triangles and shards. Place the paper back over the chocolate and tap firmly to break it up. Refrigerate until ready to use.

Cut off the domed tops of the cooled cake layers. Whip the ganache with the butter for 1 minute until lightened, but be careful not to over-whip or the mixture will separate. It's also crucial that the ganache is at room temperature and not too firm or too thin.

Place the first cake layer on a cake stand or cake board and spread a layer of ganache on top. Repeat with the next layer. Apply a thin crumb coat layer (see pages 22–23) around the outsides. Allow to set for 1 hour on the countertop or 30 minutes in the fridge. Add a final thicker layer of ganache around the sides and top.

While the ganache is still soft on the cake, decorate with the chocolate shards. The heat from your hands will melt the chocolate and leave fingerprints, so use tongs or clean tweezers to press the shards into the top of the cake. Serve immediately or refrigerate and bring back to room temperature when ready to serve.

SPRINKLE EXPLOSION

Sprinkles have always been great for livening up cupcakes, so how about completely encrusting a layer cake with them? It may sound crazy, but this idea offers such a simple way of making your layer cake scream for attention. You will need a lot of sprinkles, but almost any variety will work for this idea, and it's great for combining all your odds and ends to use them up. And as if that wasn't enough, the fun continues inside...

funfetti cake

150 g (5½ oz) brightly coloured polka dot sprinkles

3 batches Ultimate Sponge Cake batter (see page 11), each flavoured with 1 tsp vanilla extract

1 quantity Simple Syrup (see page 17), flavoured with 2 tsp vanilla extract

frosting & decoration

1 batch Italian Meringue Buttercream (see page 14), flavoured with 2 tsp vanilla extract

500 g (1 lb 2 oz) sprinkles

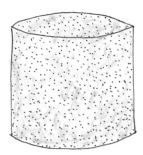

Funfetti sponge

Preheat the oven to 160°C (325°F). Grease and line three 20-cm (8-in) round cake tins.

Add the polka dot sprinkles to the cake batter and mix them through until they are evenly distributed. Divide the batter equally into three prepared cake tins and bake 45–50 minutes until a cocktail stick inserted into the centre of each cake comes out clean. Leave the cakes to cool in the tins for 20 minutes, then turn out onto a wire rack and leave to cool completely.

Level the tops of the cakes using a large serrated knife or cake leveller. Brush each sponge cake layer with vanilla-flavoured simple syrup.

You'll need two 20-cm (8-in) cake boards for this project. These are essential to this decoration technique as they allow you to pick up the cake and move it around, so you can apply the sprinkles to it evenly. Spread one of the cake boards with a little buttercream, then place the first cake layer onto the board. Apply an even layer of buttercream on the top of this layer, then carefully position the next sponge cake layer on top. Continue in this way until all the layers are stacked.

Crumb coat the assembled cake (see pages 22–23). Chill in the fridge for 30 minutes, then apply the final, thicker layer of buttercream. Now chill for 1–2 hours until the frosting is totally firm.

Follow the steps on page 71 to decorate the cake with sprinkles.

ENCRUSTING WITH SPRINKLES

1 Carefully pour your sprinkles onto a large baking sheet and spread them out across the sheet so that they form an even layer.

2 Using the hot-knife method (see page 23), dip a large angled metal spatula into hot water and smooth the frosting around the sides of the cake until the surface is slightly melted and tacky to the touch.

3 Place a cake board on top of the cake, then pick up the cake with one hand underneath and one hand on top.

4 Turn the cake on its side and roll it in the sprinkles, rotating and shaking the tray to distribute the sprinkles if necessary. (This is why the cake needs to be chilled until firm prior to decorating – to make sure that it holds its shape as you encrust the sides.)

5 Once you have an even covering on the sides of the cake, set down the cake on a flat surface. Remove the cake board from the top of the cake and hot-knife the top surface as you did the sides.

6 Make some space in the tray for a small upturned bowl. Sit the cake on this bowl. Now cover the top of the cake with sprinkles. Add extra sprinkles to gappy patches on the sides and top. Brush off excess sprinkles where necessary.

WILD THING

This striking cake is simple to make and shows how you can create exciting patterns by changing the way in which you put cake batter into a tin. The recipe creates a thin batter, which is essential for allowing the stripes to form.

chocolate orange cake

8 eggs
500 g (1 lb 2 oz) caster sugar
200 ml (7 fl oz) plus 3 tbsp milk
500 ml (18 fl oz) sunflower oil
950 g (2 lb 2 oz) self-raising flour
2 tsp baking powder
Pinch of salt
Grated zest of 1 orange
Orange food colouring paste
50 g (1¾ oz) cocoa powder, sieved

filling & frosting

½ batch dark chocolate Ganache
(see page 15)
½ batch Italian Meringue Buttercream
(see page 14), flavoured with the
grated zest of 1 orange and
1 drop orange extract
Icing sugar, for dusting
250 g (9 oz) ready-to-use
black fondant

*Chocolate & orange
tiger stripes*

Preheat the oven to 160°C (325°F). Grease and line three 20-cm (8-in) round cake tins. Put the eggs, sugar, milk, oil and half the flour into the bowl of an electric stand mixer and beat until just combined. Add the remaining flour, baking powder, and salt and mix until smooth. Divide the batter into two. Fold the orange zest and a little orange food colouring into one portion, and the cocoa powder and 3 tbsp milk into the other.

Spoon 3 tbsp of the orange batter into the centre of each cake tin. Spoon 3 tbsp of the chocolate batter directly onto the centre of the previous circle of batter. Continue to spoon alternating batters in 3-tbsp portions into the centre of the previous circle of batter until all the batter is used. Don't spread the batter or tap the tins – the drops of batter pushing previous ones down and outwards create the layering effect. Bake for 40–50 minutes.

Level the tops of the cooled cakes. Put 5 tbsp buttercream into a piping bag. Place one layer on a cake stand or cake board and pipe a border of buttercream around the top edge. Spread a layer of ganache inside this dam. Place the next cake layer on top and repeat the process. Apply a thin layer of buttercream to the outside in a crumb coat (see pages 22–23).

Divide the remaining buttercream into two portions, one using two-thirds of the buttercream and the other, one-third. Tint the large portion orange. Using an angled spatula, apply a 7-cm (2¾-in) band of plain buttercream around the bottom of the cake sides. Cover the rest of the cake in orange buttercream. Use a dough scraper or large angled spatula to smooth the buttercream, which will cause the icing shades to blend into each other.

Dust your work surface with icing sugar. Roll out the black fondant to a thickness of about 3 mm (⅛ in). Use a sharp knife to cut stripes of different widths and lengths that taper to a point at one end. Position these across the cake, up the sides and across the top, gently pressing them into place on the buttercream.

OREO LOVE

There's no hiding that this one is for serious Oreo lovers. From the shimmering decoration to the Oreos hiding inside the cake layers, to the added decadence of a cookie-dough filling, this cake is total indulgence. Who can resist when it tastes this good?

vanilla oreo cake

2 batches Ultimate Sponge Cake batter (see page 11), each flavoured with 1 tsp vanilla extract
Approximately 28 oreos
1 quantity Simple Syrup (see page 17), flavoured with 2 tsp vanilla extract

cookie-dough filling

100 g (3½ oz) unsalted butter, softened
100 g (3½ oz) dark or light brown sugar
100 g (3½ oz) plain flour
Pinch of salt
2 tbsp milk
50 g (1¾ oz) chocolate chips

chocolate frosting

1 batch Classic Buttercream (see page 14), flavoured with 2 tsp vanilla extract
¼ batch dark chocolate Ganache (see page 15)

oreo decoration

Approximately 20 Oreos
Edible metallic lustre dust

Preheat the oven to 160°C (325°F). Grease and line four 20-cm (8-in) round cake tins. Spread enough batter in the tins to just cover the bottoms. Press seven Oreos across the surface in each tin. Divide the remaining batter between the tins and spread over the Oreos. Bake for 25–30 minutes.

For the cookie-dough filling, beat together the butter and brown sugar until very pale and fluffy. The longer you beat, the less gritty the sugar will be. Mix in the flour and salt. Put half the buttercream into a medium-sized bowl. Add the other half to the cookie-dough mix and beat to combine. Beat in the milk to loosen the mixture if necessary. Stir in the chocolate chips by hand with a large spoon or spatula. Beat the ganache and remaining buttercream together until smooth.

Level the tops of the cake layers. Fill a piping bag with half of the ganache buttercream and cut a medium or large hole (of approximately 1 cm /½ in) across the tip or fit the bag with a plain tip. Place the first cake layer on a cake stand or cake board and brush with syrup. Pipe a ganache buttercream border around the top edge and spread an even amount of cookie-dough buttercream inside this dam using an angled spatula. Place the next layer on top and repeat the process.

If you have any ganache left in the piping bag, squeeze it onto the cake and crumb coat it (see pages 22–23), using extra ganache from the bowl if necessary. Chill for 30 minutes. Apply the final, thicker layer of ganache and smooth it with a dough scraper or a large offset metal spatula.

Dust the remaining Oreos with metallic lustre dust using a small (food-only) paintbrush. Press these into the sides of the cake while the buttercream is still soft. Take the last Oreos and insert a cocktail stick through the buttercream centre. Pierce them into the top of the cake.

75

PIÑATA CAKE

You can fill the centre of this cake with pretty much any small candy or sprinkles. It is so simple to make, yet is a delight to cut open, creating a spectacular reveal and inspiring a chorus of 'oohs' and 'ahhs!'

coconut cake

6 tbsp desiccated coconut
250 ml (9 fl oz) coconut milk
3 batches Ultimate Sponge Cake batter (see page 11)
1 quantity Simple Syrup (see page 17), flavoured with 1 tsp vanilla extract or the seeds from ½ vanilla pod

coconut frosting & decoration

1 batch Classic Buttercream (see page 14)
150 ml (5 fl oz) coconut cream
150 g (5½ oz) coconut flakes or desiccated coconut

filling

100 g (3½ oz) candy or sprinkles

triple coconut

Preheat the oven to 160°C (325°F). Grease and line three 20-cm (8-in) round cake tins.

Place the desiccated coconut and coconut milk into a small saucepan set over a medium heat until barely simmering. Take the saucepan off the heat and allow the mixture to cool.

Mix the cooled rehydrated coconut into the cake batter and divide the mixture between the three prepared tins. Bake for 40–45 minutes.

Level off the tops of the three cooled cake layers using a large serrated knife or cake leveller. Cut each layer in half horizontally to create six layers.

Beat the coconut cream into the buttercream until smooth.

Follow the steps on page 79 to assemble the cake. You'll need a round pastry cutter with a diameter of approximately 7.5 cm (3 in) for hollowing out the centre.

Once assembled, crumb coat the cake (see pages 22–23). Chill in the fridge for 30 minutes, then apply the final, thicker layer of buttercream to the cake.

Now, decorate your cake with a pretty layer of coconut flakes. You might want to toast the flakes first. If you would like to, spread them out on a baking sheet and grill for 30 seconds or so. Keep an eye on the flakes so they don't burn, which can happen very quickly. Allow to cool completely, then sprinkle the toasted or untoasted flakes of coconut over the frosting, and press them into the sides of the cake with your hands.

CREATING A HIDDEN HOLLOW

1 Using the round pastry cutter (see page 76), cut out a hole from the centre of all but two layers. To do this, first cut a single layer, then place it on top of an uncut layer and align the layers. Push the cutter through the hole in the top layer to cut the bottom one so that the hole in the bottom layer is in the same position as it is in the top layer. Do this twice more so you have four cut layers.

2 Brush the sponges with syrup. Place one of the uncut layers onto a cake board or a cake stand and apply an even layer of buttercream over it. Next, carefully place a layer with a hole on top and apply an even layer of buttercream onto the top of that layer. Make sure you don't get any buttercream inside the ring in the middle.

3 Repeat step 2 with the remaining ring layers. Be very careful when you move the layers around as they will be weakened by the hole in the middle.

4 Pour your chosen candy into the hole in the centre of the cake. Now apply another even layer of buttercream and place the final uncut layer on top to seal everything in.

BILLION LAYER CAKE

OK, so it may not be a billion layers, but who's counting? This is very much a layer cake, but quite different to the others in this book due to how it is made. I'm not going to lie – this is a labour-intensive process so you'll need some patience. The flavour of this cake is rich and the texture dense, so a little goes a long way.

matcha & lemon cake

500 g (1 lb 2 oz) unsalted butter, softened
400 g (14 oz) caster sugar
10 eggs, separated
250 g (9 oz) plain flour
Grated zest of 2 lemons
3 tbsp powdered matcha, sieved
100 g (3½ oz) unsalted butter, melted

white chocolate frosting

150 g (5½ oz) white chocolate chips or, if using a block, chopped finely
75 ml (2½ fl oz) sour cream
Grated zest of ¼ lemon

Preheat the grill to a medium-high setting. Position the oven shelf in the centre of the oven. Line the bottom of two 15-cm (6-in) round cake tins and grease the sides.

In a large mixing bowl, beat the butter and half of the caster sugar using an electric handblender until the mixture is very light and fluffy. Add the egg yolks and beat well until combined.

Start whisking the egg whites in the large bowl of an electric stand mixer set to a medium speed. When foamy, gradually add the remaining caster sugar and continue to whisk until stiff, smooth peaks form. Add a couple of large spoonfuls of the egg whites to the creamed mixture and beat through. Gently fold the flour and egg whites through the mixture in four alternating batches. Be careful not to overmix.

Divide the batter between two bowls and fold the lemon zest into one, and the matcha powder into the other. Spread 75 g (2¾ oz) of the matcha mix into the bottom of each tin and use the back of a spoon to smooth it out evenly across the surface of each tin. Place the tins under the grill for approximately 4 minutes for this first layer. You are looking for the layer to become golden brown and springy. It can turn very quickly, so keep an eye on this. Remove from the grill and brush with melted butter.

Spread 75 g (2¾ oz) of the lemon mix on top of the grilled layer in each tin and put the tins back under the grill for 3–4 minutes. The mixture will melt as you spread it and that's fine.

Continue this process of alternating layer of batter/grill/brush with butter until the batter fills the tins (you may have a little leftover batter). You may need to lower the shelf away from the grill half-way through the

Matcha & lemon cake

process as the cake becomes taller and inches closer to the grill. Depending on your grill, the time each layer takes to cook may vary, so use your own judgment as to when the cake is cooked but avoid overcooking as this will create a dry, dense cake. Cool in the tins for 20 minutes, then turn out onto a wire rack and cool completely.

To make the frosting, place the white chocolate into a heatproof glass or ceramic bowl and microwave on a medium setting for 30-second bursts. Once just about melted, stir through the sour cream until combined. Microwave the mixture for 10 seconds or so if any pieces of chocolate remain whole. (This process can also be done using a double boiler – see page 66). Stir through the lemon zest and allow the mixture to set to room temperature.

The tops of the cakes may be uneven but you don't want to cut them off because it would ruin the internal layered pattern. Place the first cake onto a cake stand or board and spread a very thin layer of the ganache – just enough to create a level surface for the next cake and not too much to interfere visually with the pattern when the cake is sliced. Position the second layer on top, then spread a thin layer of ganache over the top and sides of the cake using an angled metal spatula. This is a crumb coat of sorts, except there are no crumbs to catch! Apply a slightly thicker second layer, but the aim is to have barely enough to cover the cake; otherwise the frosting will overwhelm the delicate flavours.

THE GIFT

Making a bow of gumpaste provides a simple way of dressing up a cake for a birthday. The bow can be made in any colour so it is ideal as an adaptable decoration. It can be made in advance to save time – store it in an airtight container with a sachet of food-safe silica gel to keep it dry.

prepared cake

20-cm (8-in) square layered cake, filled, crumb coated and covered in a smooth layer of Classic Buttercream (see pages 10–25 for guidance)

bow decoration

Food colouring paste
250 g (9 oz) white gumpaste
Cornflour, for dusting
Small amount of Simple Syrup (see page 17) or edible glue

Make the bow in advance. Knead a small amount of your chosen food colour into the gumpaste until smooth and pliable. Divide the gumpaste into two equal portions. Wrap one tightly in cling film to stop it from drying out.

Dust your work surface with cornflour. You can use icing sugar but cornflour has a finer texture and is far better at combating sticking with gumpaste. Using a medium nonstick rolling pin, roll out the gumpaste to a thickness of 3 mm (1/8 in). You are aiming for a long rectangle that is approximately 38 cm (15 in) long and 15 cm (6 in) wide. Cut the edges with a sharp knife to neaten the rectangle.

Fold each of the long edges in towards the centre by approximately 5 mm (1/4 in). Locate the centre of the length of the rectangle. At this point, pinch the long edges of the rectangle in towards the centre of the width to create a gather. Now pinch in either end of the rectangle in the same way.

Brush a small dab of edible glue or syrup onto the gather at the middle of the length. Now fold over the two lengths on either side of the central gather to make the bow loops. Ensure the loops are of the same length. When you bring the ends of the loops to meet at the central gather, pinch the ends together and press them into the edible glue or syrup to fix them in place. (Note that you have the back of the bow facing towards you at the moment.)

You now need a rectangle of gumpaste to cover the central gather. Dust your work surface once again with cornflour and roll out a length of gumpaste to the same thickness as previously. Aim for a rectangle that's approximately 14 cm (5½ in) long and 10 cm (4 in) wide. Fold in the two long edges to meet at the centre. Pinch in either end of the rectangle. Place this rectangle beneath the bow, placing the central gather on the bow on the centre of the length of this rectangle. Brush a small dab of

edible glue or syrup onto both pinched ends of the rectangle and wrap it around the centre of the bow. Press to fix in place.

Turn over the bow so that the front of it is facing upwards. Scrunch up some clean paper towels and carefully insert them into the loops of the bow to help keep their shape. Allow to dry overnight in a cool, dry place. Reserve the remaining gumpaste, tightly wrapped in cling film, for use the next day.

When you are ready to decorate your cake, use the remaining gumpaste and repeat the first steps of the process for making the bow until you have folded the long edges in towards the centre. You now have a long ribbon. Cut the ribbon strip in half. Cut one end on each strip at an angle.

Brush a small dab of edible glue or syrup in the middle of the top of the cake and on each front corner. Drape the ribbon tails (with the angled cuts) so that they fall over the front corners of the cake and press them onto the middle of the cake to fix in place.

Brush a small dab of edible glue or sugar syrup onto the centre of the ribbon tails and press the bow on top to fix it in place, covering the joins beneath.

Simple sponge with classic buttercream

GRAPHIC HEART CAKE

Want to tell someone you love them? Then how about this supercool design? It will give you practise in handling fondant and is great for covering up a bad frosting job. This technique would also work well with other bold shapes, such as circles or stars, and creates a strikingly clean, graphic style.

prepared cake

20-cm (8-in) round layered cake, filled, crumb coated and covered in a smooth layer of frosting (see pages 10–25 for guidance)

heart decorations

800 g (1 lb 12 oz) ready-to-use white fondant
Food colouring paste
Icing sugar, for dusting
Small amount of Simple Syrup (see page 17) or edible glue

Take about 50 g (1¾ oz) of the fondant and knead in a small amount of your chosen food colouring paste until smooth and pliable. Dust your work surface with icing sugar. Using a nonstick rolling pin, roll out the fondant to a thickness of approximately 3 mm (⅛ in). Cut out three heart shapes using a heart-shaped cutter that has a 3.5 cm (1⅜ in) diameter. (You could cut out more coloured hearts if you prefer.) Put to one side.

Take the remaining white fondant and roll it out to the same thickness as before on your newly dusted work surface. Cut out hearts with the cutter until you have enough to cover the entire cake. Set to one side and allow to dry for a couple of hours, which will make it easier to pick up and handle the fondant shapes.

To decorate the cake, use a small (food-only) paintbrush to dab a small amount of edible glue or simple syrup onto the back of a white heart and gently apply it to the side of the cake at the bottom. Apply more white hearts in the same way, moving around the bottom edge, then start on the next row up. In this row, apply one of the coloured hearts to the side of the cake in place of one of the white ones. In the next two rows, apply the remaining two coloured hearts above the coloured heart in the previous row to create a vertical line of coloured hearts. Make the final row all white. It's fine if the top row of hearts overlaps the top edge of the cake a little.

Fondant hearts

TUMBLING ICED COOKIES

Using iced cookies is an unexpected way to decorate a cake. People will enjoy pulling the cookies off the cake to nibble while the cake is being sliced. This recipe yields extra cookies to allow for mishaps and experiments.

prepared cake

20-cm (8-in) round layered cake, filled, crumb coated and covered in a smooth layer of fondant (see pages 10–25 for guidance)

cookies

200 g (7 oz) unsalted butter, softened
200 g (7 oz) caster sugar
Flavouring: seeds from 1 vanilla pod; or grated zest of 1 orange or lemon; or replace 50 g (1¾ oz) of the flour with 50 g (1¾ oz) cocoa powder
1 egg
400 g (14 oz) plain flour

icing

1 batch Royal Icing (see page 16)
Food colouring pastes

Flavoured iced cookies

To make the cookies, blend together the butter, sugar, and flavouring in a large bowl until creamy. Do not beat until fluffy as this will introduce too much air into the mixture and cause the cookies to spread when baked. Beat in the egg until combined, then mix in the flour until a dough forms. Divide into two portions, flatten each to a thickness of about 2.5 cm (1 in), and wrap in cling film. Refrigerate for 30 minutes.

Place the dough between two sheets of parchment paper and, using a large rolling pin, roll out the dough to a thickness of 5 mm (¼ in). Cut out flower shapes using cookie cutters in varying sizes. Place these on baking trays lined with parchment paper. Try to keep the larger shapes on one sheet and the smaller ones on another for even baking. You can knead and re-roll scraps of dough once before they become unusable. Carefully insert a kebab stick, blunt-end first, into three of the larger shapes to prepare your cookie cake toppers. Refrigerate for 30 minutes and preheat the oven to 160°C (325°F).

Bake the cookies for 8–12 minutes (depending on their sizes) until golden brown around the edges. Transfer to a wire rack to cool.

Decorate the cookies by following the instructions on page 88. Remember – the line icing needs to have the consistency of the soft peaks of meringue, yet be firm enough to hold its shape, while the flood icing should have the consistency of double cream.

When the icing on your cookies is dry, use dots of royal icing on the backs to apply them to the sides of the cake. Take the three cookies on sticks and insert them into the top of the cake in a staggered formation.

TO ICE THE COOKIES

1 Divide the royal icing equally between two bowls. Add ½ tsp water to one and mix it in well for the line icing. Now slowly mix 1–2 tsp water into the icing in the other bowl until it has the correct consistency for flood icing (see page 86).

2 Colour the icings with colouring pastes. Spoon each colour into a disposable piping bag. Cut a 5-mm (¼-in) hole into the tips of the bags containing flood icing and a 3-mm (⅛-in) hole into the tips of the line icing bags.

3 Outline the cookies with the line icing, making sure the lines are of an even thickness that is a size that will contain the flood icing when it is added later.

4 Allow the outlines to air dry for around 30 minutes, then fill with the flood icing.

5 Pop any air bubbles right away with the tip of a kebab stick. Dry out the cookies overnight or place them in a barely warm oven to dry out (the baking tray should be no more than only just too hot to hold with bare hands, or you will ruin the icing colour).

6 Add details with the thick line icing and allow to dry for at least 1 hour. You can switch over to a piping bag fitted with a fine tip at this stage, or thin down excess icing to fill extra cookies. The quantity of icing used will depend on your final cookie designs.

HAND-PAINTED SIMPLICITY

Painting a fondant-covered cake with food colour is an easy way to decorate a cake. You need only a handful of tools and your imagination, so start with this simple design and work your way up to more detailed projects, or let the kids loose on a plain covered cake, turning their doodles into something special.

prepared cake

20-cm (8-in) round layered cake, filled, crumb coated and covered in a smooth layer of fondant (see pages 10–25 for guidance)

painted decoration

Food colouring pastes
Vodka or water

Place a dab of each food colour paste onto a clean (food-only) palette or plate, spaced apart to allow room for mixing. To turn the paste into paint, mix in a little vodka or water to create a flowing consistency. Depending on how much liquid you use, the intensity of colour will vary (which makes working with this technique a lot like using watercolours). Vodka is preferable as the alcohol content evaporates fast, avoiding the melting of sugar in the fondant. However, water can be used – just be very careful not to apply too much wet paint to the cake as it will run and take a long time to dry.

Once you have mixed some colours, test the results on a scrap of fondant if you have it and adjust the colours if necessary by adding more colouring paste or vodka.

Start at the bottom edge of the side of the cake. Paint a large circle using a small (food-only) paintbrush in a smooth continuous line. (You can go over the line once it is dry to make it more defined.) Move around the bottom edge of the cake, painting the large circles, alternating the colours, if you like. Pay attention when you start to approach the first circle and try to make your circles fit neatly in the remaining space on that row. If the joining space is too small, it can always become the back of the cake and you can paint a column of smaller circles as a seam.

Move up to the next row and continue the circles. Make them all the same size. Don't worry if your circles are wonky – it adds to the hand-painted charm and it is more important that they are similar in size.

Once the sides are covered in large circles, go back and add smaller circles inside the outer circles with alternating colours. Finally, finish with a dot in the middle of each circle.

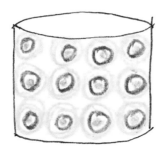

easy decoration

91

CLASSIC ROSE

Roses and hearts are a match made in heaven and this cake has both in abundance. The heart shape is cleverly made by putting a square cake together with two halves of a round cake, so no special tin is needed. Once you've mastered the pulled-rose technique, establish your own little production line to churn them out – it's surprisingly relaxing.

prepared cake

20-cm (8-in) round layered cake, levelled and filled
20-cm (8-in) square layered cake, levelled and filled

ganache

1 batch white or dark chocolate Ganache (see page 15)

rose decoration

Food colouring paste
1.5 kg (3 lb 5 oz) ready-to-use white fondant
Vegetable fat
½ batch Royal Icing (see page 16)
Icing sugar, for dusting

Ganache covered
sponge

Make the roses in advance. You'll need a few clear plastic sleeves. Knead the colour evenly through the fondant. Take 1 kg (2 lb 4 oz) of the coloured fondant, wrap it tightly in cling film and set it aside for covering the cake. Returning to the remaining fondant, pinch off a piece that weighs approximately 40 g (1½ oz), split this into five equal pieces and roll these between your palms into balls. Wrap up the remaining fondant tightly in cling film. Now follow the technique shown on page 95 to transform these five balls of coloured fondant into a rose decoration.

Use this process to make all of the roses – approximately 20 will be enough to cover the top of the cake. You may need more, depending on how thickly you make the roses and their final sizes. Leave them to dry overnight, then store them in an airtight container with a sachet of food-safe silica gel to keep them dry until you need to use them.

When you are ready to assemble the cake, cut the round cake in half vertically. Using a medium angled metal spatula, apply a thin layer of frosting to the cut sides of the two semicircular cakes and press one onto a side of the square cake. Now press the other semicircular cake onto an adjacent side of the square cake (not the side that is opposite the side the first semicircular cake is attached to). It is important to have levelled and filled both the square and round cakes to the same height so that the heart shape is created without a step in height between them.

Using an offset angled spatula, apply a thin crumb coat with the ganache. Chill in the fridge for 30 minutes. Apply a final, thicker layer of ganache to the cake. Chill in the fridge for 30 minutes.

Dust your work surface with icing sugar. Using a nonstick rolling pin, roll out the reserved coloured fondant to a thickness of 3 mm (⅛ in). Use it to cover the cake (see page 24).

To decorate the cake, colour the royal icing the same colour as the roses. Place it into a piping bag and cut a large hole across the tip that is approximately 1 cm (½ in) in diameter, or fit the bag with a small plain tip. Consider where you wish to position your roses, then pipe a small blob of royal icing onto the back of a rose and gently press it into position on top of the cake to fix it in place. Repeat the process until the top of the cake is covered in roses. Leave to set for 1 hour.

TIP: To cover the entire cake in fondant roses, you'll need approximately 75 of them. Use 1.5 kg (3 lb 5 oz) fondant. When applying the roses to the cake, start on the sides, at the bottom edges, and work around the cake until you have a row. Move on to the row above once the piped icing has set. The roses are heavy, so while the icing is setting, if they slide a little, use cocktail sticks inserted a little way into the cake beneath each rose to support them. Remove the cocktail sticks once set.

PULLED ROSE TECHNIQUE

1 Lightly grease the insides of the plastic sleeve. Place the five balls of fondant between the greased plastic sheets.

2 With your thumb, press down on each ball to flatten it out.

3 Using a side-to-side movement, smooth one edge of each flattened ball to create a petal with a thin edge and a thicker base.

4 Take one petal and roll it into a spiral. The thin edge is the top of the petal and the thicker edge is the bottom.

5 Take another petal and wrap it around the spiral, covering the seam. Take the next petal and tuck the edge slightly inside the previous petal before wrapping around. Repeat this until you have wrapped all of the petals around the central spiral.

6 Tease out the petal edges with your fingertips so they ripple and curl. Use a metal spatula to cut off excess fondant from the base and stand the rose on its base to dry. Divide 40 g (1½ oz) fondant into five pieces, roll into balls, and begin at step 1. Repeat until you have enough roses to cover the cake top.

PEARL CASCADE

Chic and glamorous, this cake is the perfect example of how you can transform the simplest of materials into something stunning. Anyone can roll a ball of fondant, so if you're looking for an easy decoration that creates instant elegance, give this one a try.

prepared cake

20-cm (8-in) round layered cake, filled, crumb coated and covered in a smooth layer of fondant (see pages 10–25 for guidance)

pearl decoration

500 g (1 lb 2 oz) ready-to-use ivory-tinted fondant
Edible pearl lustre dust
Vodka or water
½ batch Royal Icing (see page 16)

Fondant covered sponge

Pinch off a small piece of fondant the size of a pea and roll it in the palms of your hands to create a pearl shape. Place it on a baking sheet lined with wax paper. Repeat this technique, rolling balls of varying sizes, but try to keep as close to the original pea size as possible. If a ball looks too big, pinch away a little fondant and roll again. Keep the block of fondant well covered in cling film while you do this to prevent it from drying out.

By the time you have got to the end of the block of fondant, the early pearls should have dried a little. Starting with these, use a medium or large (food-only) paintbrush to dust the balls with the edible pearl lustre dust, pushing and rolling them around until they have an even sheen.

Brush the top of the cake with a small amount of vodka or water (just enough to make the top a little sticky). Cover the top with pearls so that they are glued to the top, moistening the fondant on the cake again if it dries as you work.

Fill a disposable piping bag with royal icing and cut a small hole that is approximately 3 mm (⅛ in) across the tip, or fit the bag with a small, plain piping tip. Pipe a small dot of royal icing on one of the remaining pearls and attach it to the top edge of the cake. Continue in this way, attaching pearls to the top edge and sides of the cake in a cascading design. Build up the centre of the top of the cake by piling on more pearls and attaching them with royal icing.

Finish by attaching a band of ribbon around the bottom of the cake, if desired. Glue together the ends of the ribbon where they meet at the back of the cake with a dab of royal icing or edible glue applied with a small (food-only) paintbrush.

SCALLOP PATCHWORK

A combination of bright colours and texture create an eye-catching contemporary decoration on this pretty cake. The technique itself is super simple – it is the colours that make it come alive. This idea is a modern take on the patchwork quilt and it would make a great addition to any funky celebration.

prepared cake

20-cm (8-in) round layered cake, filled, crumb coated and covered in a smooth layer of frosting (see pages 10–25 for guidance)

scallop decoration

800 g (1 lb 12 oz) ready-to-use white fondant
Icing sugar, for dusting
Food colouring pastes
Small amount of Simple Syrup (see page 17) or edible glue

To make the fondant scallops, divide the fondant into as many equal portions as the number of colours you wish to use. Knead a small amount of colouring paste into each portion until smooth and pliable. Tightly wrap the variously coloured fondant portions in cling film, reserving one ball to use right away.

Dust your work surface with icing sugar. Using a medium-sized nonstick rolling pin, roll out the fondant to a thickness of approximately 3 mm (1/8 in). Use a round pastry cutter with a diameter of 3 cm (1¼ in) to cut out discs of fondant, working on one colour at a time. Set the discs to one side for a couple of hours to dry, which will make it easier to pick them up and apply them to the cake.

When you are ready to apply the fondant discs to the cake, use a food-only small paintbrush to dab a small quantity of edible glue or syrup onto the back of one disc. Gently apply the disc to the side of the cake at the bottom edge. Apply another disc right next to the first in the same way. Continue to work all the way around the bottom edge of the cake.

Now start on the next row. Take the first disc for this row and position it over the join between two discs in the row below. This overlap is what creates the scallop shape. Continue working in this way until it's time to apply the last row of scallops. Trim off approximately one-third of each disc, ensuring they are trimmed identically, then attach them to the cake in the same way.

Multi coloured fondant scallops

98

CORSAGE CASCADE

Designed to mimic the ruffled ripples of flowers on a corsage, these gorgeous flower accessories add a burst of colour and interest to a cake. Adapt the colours to suit the occasion for a pretty feminine style or a celebratory fanfare.

prepared cake

20-cm (8-in) round layered cake, filled, crumb coated and covered in a smooth layer of fondant (see pages 10–25 for guidance)

corsage decoration

150 g (5½ oz) white gumpaste
150 g (5½ oz) ready-to-use white fondant
Food colouring pastes
Icing sugar, for dusting
Small amount of Simple Syrup (see page 17) or edible glue

To make the corsages, you'll need a series of four round pastry cutters, ranging in size from 3–10 cm (1¼–4 in). Have these ready before you begin. You'll also need a frilling tool (see page 123). The frilling technique takes a bit of practise, so try it out on a strip of fondant first to get the hang of it, but don't worry about it not being perfect as you are aiming for a distressed edge.

Knead the gumpaste and fondant together until smooth and pliable. Divide it into two to three portions (depending on the colours of your design) and colour each one using a food colouring paste. Tightly wrap the fondant/gumpaste portions, reserving one ball to use right away.

Dust your work surface with icing sugar. Using a medium nonstick rolling pin, roll out the mixture to a thickness of approximately 3 mm (⅛ in). Cut out three discs using the three cutters that are largest in size. Take the largest of these discs and, using the frilling tool, roll around the edges to thin and ruffle. Repeat with the other two discs.

Using a small (food-only) paintbrush, apply a small amount of edible glue or syrup to the middle of the back of the largest disc, leaving a 2-cm (¾-in) gap around the edges. Attach the ruffled disc to the side of the cake, starting near the bottom edge. Apply a little more glue if needed to fix it in place.

Add the disc that is the next-size down to the middle of the first in the same way. Now repeat with the smallest of the three ruffled discs. When all three are attached, tease the edges of each disc with your fingertips to emphasise the ruffles.

Using a small round cutter with a diameter of 3 cm (1¼ in), cut out five more discs and ruffle the edges as before with the frilling tool. Fold each

Gumpaste corsage

one in half into a semicircular shape, and then half again so that you end with a fan shape (see picture, left).

Using a small paintbrush, apply a small amount of edible glue or syrup to the centre of the corsage you have applied to the cake. Gently press the ruffled fans onto the centre so that they sit side-by-side. Once they are fixed, tease out the edges to make the corsage look fuller.

Repeat this process with the remaining fondant/gumpaste mixture to make two more corsages. Feel free to vary the sizes of the corsages if you like by changing the sizes of the cutters you use to cut the discs. Apply the corsages to the cake in a sweeping shape up the side.

EMERGENCY STRIPES

This cake has a secret. Do you want to know what it is? Well, despite it looking pretty cool, it is decorated using what has to be the easiest way of dressing up a cake – no skills required, honestly! This idea came to me once when I found myself without my usual supplies and had to improvise. The pleasure of seeing the fantastic result was enhanced only by how stress-free the process was!

prepared cake

20-cm (8-in) round layered cake, filled, crumb coated and covered in a smooth layer of frosting (see pages 10–25 for guidance)

stripe decoration

1.5 kg (3 lb 5 oz) ready-to-use white fondant
Yellow food colouring paste
Icing sugar, for dusting
Small amount of Simple Syrup (see page 17) or edible glue

Divide the fondant into three equal portions and colour each portion a different shade of yellow (or whichever colour you have chosen – or work the strips in different colours if you prefer). Pinch off 100 g (3½ oz) from each portion. Wrap the remainder of each portion tightly in cling film.

Dust your work surface with icing sugar. Using a medium nonstick rolling pin, roll out the first shade of yellow into a long rectangle that is approximately 3 mm (¹/₈ in) thick. The rectangle ideally needs to be long enough to go over two sides and the top of the cake, so aim for approximately 40 cm (16 in).

Using a sharp knife, cut long strips from the rolled fondant, making them approximately 1.5 cm (⁵/₈ in) wide. Knead and wrap up any leftovers to reuse later. Repeat this with the other two pieces of fondant. You want to have about two strips of each colour at a time – any more and they will dry out before you place them on the cake.

Lay the first strip across the cake so that it extends up one side, across the top, and down the other side. Trim the ends to size using a sharp knife. Repeat this with the remaining strips, alternating shades and directions when you place the fondant strips. The fondant should stick to the frosting, but if the frosting has set and is no longer tacky, simply brush a little edible glue or syrup onto the cake using a clean (food-only) paintbrush before applying the strips.

Repeat this process with the remaining fondant until you can no longer see the frosting underneath. You will need to use a little edible glue or syrup toward the end to help fix the fresh fondant strips on top of the other fondant strips.

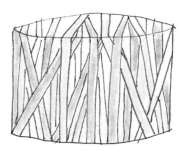

Yellow fondant stripes

LADY-IN-WAITING DOME

This layer cake with a twist was inspired by the classic Swedish princess cake, but unlike the original, this one is fairly simple – so more of a lady-in-waiting than a full-blown princess. And it tastes pretty amazing, too.

sponge cake

2 batches Ultimate Sponge Cake batter (see page 11), each flavoured with 1 tsp vanilla extract

crème pâtissière

500 ml (17 fl oz) whole milk
Seeds from 1 vanilla pod
125 g (4½ oz) caster sugar
120 g (4¼ oz) or 5 medium egg yolks
40 g (1½ oz) cornflour
100 g (3½ oz) unsalted butter, cubed

raspberry filling

500 ml (17 fl oz) double cream
50 g (1¾ oz) icing sugar, sieved
250 g (9 oz) high-quality raspberry jam
150 g (5½ oz) fresh raspberries

frosting & decoration

1 batch Classic Buttercream (see page 14), flavoured with ½ tsp almond essence
Green and deep pink food colouring pastes
500 g (1 lb 2 oz) ready-to-use white fondant
Vegetable fat

Preheat the oven to 160°C (325°F). Grease and line a 20-cm (8-in) round cake tin. Grease and flour the insides of a glass baking dish or stainless steel bowl with a diameter of 20 cm (8 in). Spread one batch of the cake batter into the prepared cake tin and bake for 45–50 minutes. Allow to cool, then cut the cake in half horizontally to create two layers.

Reduce the oven temperature to 170°C (325°F). Spread the other batch of cake batter into the bowl and bake for 45–50 minutes. The oven temperature is lower because the bowl does not insulate in the same way as a cake tin, so the baking time of the cake will depend on the bowl you use. Keep an eye on the cake while it bakes and adjust the time accordingly. Allow to almost completely cool in the bowl, then turn out onto a cooling rack.

To make the crème pâtissière, put the milk, vanilla pod seeds, and 50 g (1¾ oz) of the sugar into a saucepan and heat until just simmering. Take the saucepan off the heat and leave to cool for 5–10 minutes.

Meanwhile, in a large bowl, whisk the egg yolks, remaining sugar and cornflour until pale and thick. Slowly add the hot milk, stirring continuously. Pour the mixture back into the saucepan, gently heat to a simmer, and whisk until it has thickened. Take the saucepan off the heat and stir in the butter. Pour the custard through a fine sieve to remove any lumps. Cover the custard with cling film and refrigerate to cool.

Prepare the filling. Whip the cream until the medium firm peaks stage. Sieve in the icing sugar and fold it through until combined.

Now assemble the cake following the instructions on page 106.

To decorate the filled, layered cake, tint the almond buttercream with a little green food colouring paste and apply a thin crumb coat (see pages 22–23) to the cake. Chill in the fridge for 30 minutes.

Apply a final coat of buttercream. Don't worry too much about getting a perfect finish. Instead, focus on accentuating the dome shape by adding a little more frosting to the top or lower sides, for example.

Follow the instructions on page 95 to make 24 medium-sized deep pink roses. Place these around the edge of the cake and one at the centre of the dome.

ASSEMBLING THE DOME CAKE

1 Use a serrated knife or cake leveller to level the top of the round cake. Cut it in half horizontally to create two layers. Level the flat side of the dome so that it sits evenly.

2 Using a sharp knife, cut out the middle section. Mark a circle that is no less than 2.5 cm (1 in) in from the edge and zigzag the knife around, then cut out a shallow circle cleanly to create a thin round layer that is approximately 2.5 cm (1 in) deep. Don't worry if it breaks – it can be patched.

3 Once you have taken away this first layer, use a spoon to scoop out the rest of the cake centre of the dome. Chill the hollowed-out dome in the fridge while you layer the round cake.

4 Place the bottom layer of the round cake onto a board or cake stand. Spread a generous amount of raspberry jam across the layer. Spread an even layer of the thickened and cooled crème pâtissière and press a handful of raspberries into it. Place the next layer on top and press down gently. Spread another layer of jam, custard and berries.

5 Take the remaining crème pâtissière and fold it into the whipped cream. Fold through a handful of fresh raspberries. Remove the dome from the fridge and fill the hollow with the custard cream, leaving a small gap for the circle of cake that you cut out earlier. Press this back in place, sealing the filling inside.

6 Invert the dome so that it sits flat and place it on top of the layered round cake. Gently press down to fix it into place.

VERTICAL LAYERS

This impressive cake makes a wonderful centrepiece for a party. Nobody will be expecting the layers to be flipped on the inside, either, so by using simple techniques in an unexpected way you can create something fun.

multi-coloured sponge

3 batches Ultimate Sponge Cake batter (see page 11), flavoured to your taste
3 food colouring pastes

frosting & decoration

2 batches Classic Buttercream (see page 14), flavoured to your taste
Colourful sprinkles (optional)

This centrepiece cake sits on a large board. You'll need a piece of cardboard or hardboard that is 55 x 20 cm (22 x 8 in). Spread a thin layer of non-toxic glue onto the cardboard or hardboard and wrap it in decorative paper. Cover the paper with clear adhesive contact paper, smoothing away air bubbles as you go.

Preheat the oven to 160°C (325°F). Grease and line three 20-cm (8-in) square cake tins. Divide the cake batter between three bowls. Mix a food colour into each batch of batter to create three distinct colours. Pour each batter into its own cake tin and bake for 30–35 minutes.

Level the tops of the cooled cakes, then use a large serrated knife to cut each cake vertically into quarters, so that you end up with 12 squares of cake that are 10 x 10 cm (4 x 4 in). Using a small angled metal spatula, spread an even layer of buttercream on one side of each square.

Spread a little buttercream across the centre of the prepared board so that the cake sticks to the board. Stand the first layer about 5 cm (2 in) in from one end of the board, with the buttercream on the side that is facing toward the opposite end of the board. Into this covering of buttercream, press the second cake layer, which should have its own buttercream side facing away from the first layer, ready to receive the third layer. Use the spatula to press the cakes together and smooth out the exposed buttercream again. Repeat this technique, alternating the colours of the layers, until all are used.

Apply a crumb coat (see pages 22–23) with an angled metal spatula, then leave the cake on the worktop for 1 hour to allow the frosting to set.

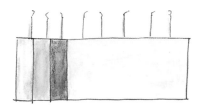

Simple party cake

Now apply the final layer of frosting (which can be coloured, if desired) and smooth it out for an even finish (see page 23). Decorate with sprinkles and/or long taper candles, if desired.

THAT'S A WRAP!

If you want to cover up a messy frosting job or give your cake a quick and stylish decorating job, this wrapped piped design is ideal. Go freestyle with squiggles or plan a piped design, but work quickly before the first pieces of piping set.

prepared cake

20-cm (8-in) round layered cake, filled, crumb coated and covered in a smooth layer of frosting (see pages 10–25 for guidance)

decoration

150 g (5½ oz) candy melts or chocolate

Cut a piece of wax paper that is long enough to wrap around the sides of the cake and deep enough to extend 2.5–5 cm (1–2 in) above the top edge of the cake.

Place the candy melts or chocolate into a medium glass or ceramic bowl and gently melt in the microwave in short bursts, stirring in between intervals. You can also melt using the double-boiler method (in a bowl set on a saucepan above simmering water – see page 66).

Pour the melted candy melts or chocolate into a piping bag. Let it cool down a little if it feels too hot and looks thin. It should have a smooth, flowing consistency. Cut a 3-mm (¹⁄₈-in) wide hole across the tip of the piping bag or fit the bag with a small plain tip.

Pipe a design across the wax paper sheet, working quickly so that the melted candy melts or chocolate sets at the same rate. Once the design is finished, check that the consistency changes from wet to firm but is still pliable. You can check this by gently lifting up the wax paper. If the design runs it needs to set a little. If it cracks, pop it into a warm oven for a minute until it is pliable again.

When the consistency is right, lift the wax paper and wrap it around the sides of the cake to press the design gently onto the surface of the cake. To do this, fix one end first and carefully wrap around until the other end joins the first. Try not to press the design too hard as it will smudge the piping. Also be confident with the placement, as you can't move and adjust the design once it touches the cake.

Depending on the room temperature, the wrap will set at different rates. If it is still soft after 15 minutes, place the cake in the fridge for 30 minutes to firm up. Gently pull away the wax paper to reveal the piped design applied to the cake.

Squiggle decoration

MINI WOOF WOOFS

These little cuties are too good to resist and great fun to make. They look best if each one is a little different, so don't worry about making them look identical and enjoy giving each dog it's own personality. You can adapt the idea to make other animals – add pointy ears and whiskers to make a cat, for example.

sponge cake

1 batch Ultimate Sponge Cake batter (see page 11), flavoured with 1 tsp vanilla extract, or any recipe of your choice
½ quantity Simple Syrup (see page 17), flavoured with 1 tsp vanilla extract

frosting & decoration

1 batch Classic Buttercream (see page 14) flavoured with 2 tsp vanilla extract or to your taste
Pale brown, beige, gray, black and red food colouring pastes
250 g (9 oz) ready-to-use white fondant
Icing sugar, for dusting

Mini dog cakes

Preheat the oven to 160°C (325°F). Grease and line a 20-cm (8-in) square cake tin. Spread the cake batter into the prepared tin. Bake for 45–50 minutes and allow to cool. You'll need nine thin, round 6-cm (2½-in) mini cake cardboards, so have these on hand.

Level the top of the cake using a large serrated knife or cake leveller. Cut the cake in half horizontally to create two layers. Using a 6-cm (2½-in) round pastry cutter, cut out eighteen rounds from the two layers of sponge. It will be quite a tight fit, so make sure you maximise the space when cutting out the rounds.

Using a small angled metal spatula, smear a little buttercream on the cake cardboards, then press one sponge circle onto each cardboard. Brush each of these first layers with a little simple syrup, then spread an even amount of buttercream over the top. Press the next layer on top and brush with a little syrup. Using a small angled metal spatula, cover each mini cake with a thin layer of buttercream. Chill for 15 minutes.

To decorate the cakes, divide the remaining buttercream into three small bowls. Add a small amount of food colouring paste to tint each portion of frosting. You want to end with a light brown, a gray and beige or cream.

Divide the fondant into two chunks, one of 125 g (4½ oz) and the other of 75 g (2¾ oz). Pinch off a piece of fondant the size of a hazelnut from the larger chunk and wrap it tightly in cling film. Knead black food colouring paste into the larger chunk to tint it black, and red into the smaller chunk to tint it a deep pink.

Place the three buttercream colours into piping bags fitted with a small star tip. Starting on the top of a mini cake, pipe strands of fur to start

forming the face using the picture to the left as a guide. Pipe short spiky dots around the sides of the cake. Repeat with the other colours on the other mini cakes.

Dust your work surface with icing sugar. Using a nonstick rolling pin, roll out the black fondant to a thickness of approximately 3 mm (⅛ in). Using a 1-cm (½-in) round pastry cutter, cut out eighteen eyes. Roll out the pink fondant and cut out nine tongues using the same cutter. Roll a tiny bit of the white fondant into a ball in the palm of your hands and press it onto the centre of a black circle. Repeat for all of the eyes.

Make noses with the remaining black fondant. Divide it into nine chunks and roll each of these into a ball. Flatten a ball in your palm and shape it into a soft triangle shape. Using the end of a paintbrush or kebab stick, indent little nostrils along the bottom edge. Repeat with the remaining balls of black-tinted fondant.

Position the eyes, nose and tongue onto the top of each cake, sliding them into the buttercream a little so that they disappear into the fur. Pipe a little extra buttercream fur around the eyes and anywhere that needs building up.

COUNT TO TEN

There are so many times when a cake in the shape of a number is needed, be it a twenty-first birthday celebration or a 'hurrah, you got eight A grades on your tests!' kind of occasion. Fancy, number-shaped cake tins certainly make life easier, but you can make any number using round and square cake tins with a little crafty carving and filling. Here's how, starting with numero uno!

sponge cake

2 batches Ultimate Sponge Cake batter (see page 11), or any recipe of your choice
1 quantity Simple Syrup (see page 17)

frosting & decoration

1 batch Classic Buttercream (see page 14) or Italian Meringue Buttercream (see page 14)
Food colouring pastes
150 g (5½ oz) ready-to-use white fondant
Icing sugar, for dusting

TIP: To make your own cake board for your number shape cake, follow the instructions on page 109 and adjust the sizing accordingly.

Preheat the oven to 160°C (325°F). Grease and line two 20-cm (8-in) square cake tins. Divide the batter equally between the tins and bake for 45–50 minutes. Allow to cool. Prepare a cake board (see tip below) if you would like to assemble this cake on a cake board.

Using a large serrated knife or cake leveller, level the tops of the cakes. Cut them in half horizontally to create four layers. Brush the sponges with syrup and stack the cake with frosting between each cake layer. Gently press down on the top layer to ensure the air is squeezed out of the stack. Scrape off any frosting that has spilled out of the sides of the cake between the cake layers. Chill in the fridge for 30 minutes.

Remove the cake from the fridge and place it on a clean work surface. Using a large serrated knife, make two parallel cuts to cut the cake into three equally sized oblongs (see the cutting template on page 156). About half way up on one oblong (labelled 'C' on the cutting template), cut the oblong in half at a 45-degree angle.

Using the positioning template on page 156 as a guide, and a little frosting to act as glue, attach oblongs 'A' and 'B' together to make an upside down 'T' shape. Add oblong 'C' (the one with the 45-degree cut) with its longest edge against the top of oblong 'B,' the angle sloping down, and the shortest edge aligned to the right-hand side of oblong 'B.'

Apply a thin layer of frosting with an angled metal spatula to crumb coat. Allow to set for 30 minutes, then apply the final, thicker layer of frosting, smoothing out any gaps to create a uniform shape with no visible joins.

To decorate the cake, knead food colouring paste into the fondant to make as many different colours as you like. Dust your work surface with icing sugar. Using a nonstick rolling pin, roll out each colour to a thickness of 3 mm (1/8 in). Using star-shaped pastry cutters of various sizes, stamp out stars in a variety of sizes and colours.

Place the stars randomly over the cake immediately, gently pressing them into place while they are still soft so that they can bend over edges where necessary.

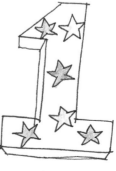

Coloured stars

I'LL HAVE FRIES WITH THAT

Love hamburgers? Love cake? Then how about a hamburger cake! This project is super fun and so easy to put together. It is guaranteed to bring smiles to everyone's faces. If this recipe is missing your favourite burger filling, get creative with fondant and food colours to create cheese slices, bacon or gherkin.

burger bun cakes

2 layers Ultimate Sponge Cake (see page 11), each flavoured with 2 tsp vanilla extract

hamburger cake

1 layer Chocolate Fudge Cake (see page 11)

frosting & decoration

1 batch Classic Buttercream (see page 14) or Italian Meringue Buttercream (see page 14), flavoured with 2 tsp vanilla extract
Food colouring pastes
White strand sprinkles

Divide the buttercream between two medium bowls. Put one bowl aside and divide the other into three equal portions. Using a small amount of food colouring paste for each portion, tint one portion red, another green and the final portion yellow. Place the four different-coloured buttercreams into piping bags. Cut a 5-mm (¼-in) diameter hole across the tips or fit with a medium plain tip.

Once the cakes are completely cooled, level the dome on one of the burger bun sponge cakes and the chocolate fudge hamburger cake layer using a serrated knife or cake leveller.

Place the levelled sponge cake layer onto a cake stand or board and pipe an even layer of the uncoloured buttercream over it, going right up to the edges of the cake layer.

Place the chocolate fudge cake hamburger layer on top and gently press down. Now, pipe the green buttercream over this cake layer to suggest lettuce. Go right to the edges and flatten the green frosting with an angled metal spatula to create the wavy look of lettuce. Add rounds of tomatoes using the red frosting, followed by strings of yellow frosting for the mustard. Remember that you will see only the frosting at the cake edges, so make sure that they spill over the edges of the chocolate layer a little bit. The middle can be messy as it will be covered by the sponge cake so will not be visible.

Position the final sponge cake layer on top, with the dome side facing upwards. Scatter a few strands of white sprinkles over the top to suggest sesame seeds.

ultimate burger

MINI STACKED TIERS

These miniature stacked cakes are easy to put together, super cute and ideal for any special occasion. Get yourself into a production line to make it easy to put them together.

mini sponge cakes

1 batch Ultimate Sponge Cake batter (see page 11), flavoured with 1 tsp vanilla extract, or any recipe of your choice
½ quantity Simple Syrup (see page 17), flavoured with 1 tsp vanilla extract

frosting & decoration

1 batch Classic Buttercream (see page 14), flavoured with 2 tsp vanilla extract or to your taste
Food colouring pastes
1 kg (2 lb 4 oz) ready-to-use white fondant
Icing sugar, for dusting
Edible glue

Yellow mini cakes

Preheat the oven to 160°C (325°F). Grease and line a 20-cm (8-in) square cake tin. Spread the batter in the cake tin. Bake for 45–50 minutes. Level the top of the cooled cake and cut it in half horizontally to create two layers.

Using a round pastry cutter with a diameter of 6 cm (2½ in), cut out twelve rounds from the two layers of sponge. Now cut another twelve rounds using a 4-cm (1½-in) round cutter. It will be a tight fit, so make sure you maximise the space when cutting out the rounds.

You will need six thin round mini cake cardboards with a diameter of 6 cm (2½ in) for the mini tier cakes. Using a small metal spatula, smear a little buttercream onto the cardboards, then press a larger round onto each cardboard.

Brush these first layers with a little simple syrup, then spread an even layer of buttercream on top. Position a large round on top of each of the cake layers on the cake cards.

Sandwich together two of the smaller cake layers with a layer of buttercream. Repeat with the remaining smaller layers. You should now have six larger tiers on cake cards and six smaller tiers without cake cards. Cover each mini cake tier with a thin layer of buttercream and chill in the fridge for 15 minutes.

Knead a small amount of food colouring paste into the fondant. Break off a chunk of coloured fondant and wrap up the rest tightly in cling film.

Dust your work surface with icing sugar. Using a nonstick rolling pin, roll out the fondant to a thickness of approximately 3 mm (⅛ in). Cut out a patch that is large enough to cover a bottom tier. Lift the patch over a bottom cake tier and smooth the top and sides with your hands. Use fondant smoothers to buff and fix the fondant in place. Trim off the

excess fondant with a sharp knife. Repeat this process until all top and bottom tiers are covered. They will be difficult to handle as they are so small, which is why chilling helps, but a lightness of touch when smoothing the fondant is also helpful.

To stack the tiers, place a smaller one on top of a larger base tier and fix it in place with a dab of buttercream or moistened fondant.

Make six small roses following the instructions on page 95. Dab a little edible glue onto the top of each mini cake and fix on a rose.

You'll need about 2.3 m (2½ yd) ribbon to decorate these cakes. Cut six lengths to fit around the bottom of the lower tiers, and six lengths to fit around the upper tiers. Wrap a length of ribbon around each tier and fix it in place with a little dab of edible glue.

RUFFLED

This spectacular ruffled cake is a wonderful example of a simple technique that creates a total wow factor. The cake can be soft and feminine in all white for a wedding or you can go all out with striking colours for a contemporary celebration. Either way, it certainly makes a bold statement.

prepared cake

20-cm (8-in) round layered cake, filled, crumb coated and covered in a smooth layer of fondant (see pages 10–25 for guidance)

ruffle decoration

400 g (14 oz) ready-to-use white fondant
400 g (14 oz) white gumpaste
Food colouring pastes
Icing sugar, for dusting
Edible glue or a little Simple Syrup (see page 17)

Multi coloured gumpaste ruffles

For this project, you will need a frilling tool, which will allow you to create the ruffles for the decoration. This tool is inexpensive and helps you to make ruffles that are dramatic and impressive.

Creating the ruffles requires quite a lot of rolling. If you have a pasta machine, I strongly recommend you use it to roll the strips of fondant nice and thin (dust the fondant with icing sugar first). If you don't have one, I suggest you get ready to settle in for a whole lot of rolling!

Knead the fondant and gumpaste together until the mixture is smooth and pliable. Divide the mixture into the number of colours you wish to use. Knead a small amount of food colouring paste into each portion and wrap each of them tightly in cling film until ready to use.

Take the portion coloured with the hue you wish your top frill to be made from. Pinch off a small piece that is the size of a lemon and wrap up the rest tightly until ready to use.

Follow the instructions on page 123 to make the ruffles and apply them to the cake. If you find during decorating the cake with the fondant ruffles, or at the end, that a ruffle is sagging downwards, apply a little more edible glue or simple syrup behind the strip to hold it in place against the cake for 1–2 seconds. Or, add cocktail sticks to hold up particularly toublesome ruffles while they dry. Make sure you remember to remove the cocktail sticks. Leave the ruffles to set and dry overnight.

MAKING AND APPLYING RUFFLES

1 Using either a pasta machine or a rolling pin and icing sugar for dusting, roll out the fondant into a long strip that is 3 mm (⅛ in) thick and 3 cm (1¼ in) wide. Aim for at least 15 cm (6 in) in length.

2 Using a sharp knife, trim the edges of the fondant strip to neaten it.

3 Take the frilling stick and roll it back and forth along one of the long edges of your strip. This will thin and ripple the fondant, creating the ruffled effect.

4 Position the cake on a cake stand, cake board or turntable. Brush a little edible glue along the plain edge of the frilled fondant strip, on the opposite side of the strip to the one that you applied the frilling stick.

5 Wrap the strip around the sides of the cake with the plain edge at the bottom and the frilled edge at the top, starting at the top edge. Gently press to stick the strip to the cake with the edible glue. Pleat and manipulate the strip to accentuate the ruffle.

6 Make another strip in the same way and attach this to the cake where you previously left off. Continue attaching ruffles in this way, moving down the sides of the cake row by row, overlapping the previous row by about 1 cm (½ in) to conceal the joins.

FLOWER MEADOW

Unashamedly feminine, this stunning cake shows the wonderful effect you can achieve by mixing flower shapes and completely covering a cake in sugar blooms. The flowers will take you the better part of a day to make. You can use whatever shape of flower cutters you have and choose your own colour scheme.

prepared cake

20-cm (8-in) square layered cake, filled, crumb coated and covered in a smooth layer of fondant (see pages 10–25 for guidance)

flower decoration

500 g (1 lb 2 oz) ready-to-use white fondant
500 g (1 lb 2 oz) white gumpaste
Food colouring pastes in 3 colours
Icing sugar
Edible dusting colours
½ batch Royal Icing (see page 16)

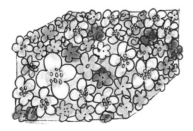

Flower covered square cake

Make the flower decorations in advance. You'll need to gather some supplies especially for making the flowers for this project, but once you have invested in and collected the items you need, you can use them again and again to recreate a variety of colour versions of this cake, and use them for other cake designs, too.

You'll need a few flower-shaped pastry cutters. Go for any shapes and sizes you like – a variety works well. You'll also need a foam pad and a ball tool to shape the petals and thin the fondant in places without damaging it, so you can achieve the delicate petal edges that help to make these flowers so pretty. You'll also need to gather up some flower formers. You will put your cut fondant flower shapes into these to give them a natural-looking curved shape, so that they don't dry flat. Use the curves of spoons to place the cut flower shapes, or cover the wells of egg boxes with cling film and place the flower shapes in these to dry.

Once you have your equipment ready, knead the fondant and gumpaste together until smooth and pliable. Divide it into three pieces and knead a small amount of food colouring paste into each piece to create three shades. Pinch off a small piece the size of a lemon from one colour. Wrap the rest tightly in cling film until ready to use. Dust your work surface with icing sugar.

Now follow steps 1–3 on page 127 to cut out and shape the flowers. Repeat the process with the remaining fondant until you have an array of flowers in three colours. If you start to run out of formers, try taking the first flowers you made off the supports, as it is likely that by the time you get to making the later flowers, the first ones will be dry enough to hold their shapes.

Allow the flowers to dry for at least a few hours until they are firm enough to hold their shapes and not fall apart when moved. At this stage you can layer up some of them by placing a smaller flower in the centre of a larger one and fixing it in place with a dab of edible glue or water.

Take the edible dusting colours. Using a small (food-only) paintbrush, gently brush a little of the dry powdered colour onto the centres of some flowers and the petal tips of others. Dust off any excess powder. This colouring step will give your flowers depth and make each one varied and interesting.

Now it's time to decorate the cake with your flowers. Place the royal icing into a piping bag and cut a small hole with a diameter of approximately 3 mm (¹⁄₈ in) across the tip, or fit the bag with a small plain tip. Follow steps A and B on page 127 to attach the flowers to the cake.

MAKING AND ATTACHING FLOWER DECORATIONS

1 Using a nonstick rolling pin, roll out the fondant to a thickness of approximately 3 mm (1/8 in). Cut out different flower shapes.

2 Now place the flower shapes on the foam pad and thin out their edges by rolling the end of a ball tool along the edges of the petals.

3 Place the flowers in the flower formers you prepared and leave them to dry with a curved shape.

A Starting at the top of the cake, attach the flowers by using a small amount of royal icing on the back to stick them to the fondant covering the cake. It is easiest to start with one flower and then add more around that starting point, expanding outwards. Make sure that the fondant underneath does not show through in patches too much. Position the flowers so that their petals overlap, hiding the fondant below.

B Once the top is covered, expand down the sides, attaching flowers in the same way. You might need to hold the flowers in place for a little longer than on the top to allow them to set if gravity starts dragging them downwards. Starting on the top before the sides also allows you to start thinning out where you put them to give a cascade effect if you find you haven't made enough flowers. Pipe little dots into the centre of some flowers to finish. Leave the royal icing to set.

24CT DECADENCE

'Complete and utter decadence' just about sums up this cake! For the ultimate in luxury, it is completely covered in gold leaf, a simple decoration that creates a sleek and chic centrepiece. Gold leaf is not cheap, but for such a knocks-your-socks-off finish for a very special occasion, it is well worth the expense. Make sure that you use only 24ct food-grade gold transfer leaf that is not mixed with an alloy, or use food-grade silver transfer leaf.

prepared cake

20-cm (8-in) round layered cake, filled, crumb coated and covered in a smooth layer of fondant (see pages 10–25 for guidance)

gold leaf decoration

10-12 sheets 24ct edible gold leaf (3 x 7.5-cm /3-in squares)
Vodka or water

Make sure that your fondant-covered cake has had time to set and is no longer soft to the touch. Using a large (food-only) paintbrush, dampen a section the size of one square of gold leaf on the side of the cake with vodka or water. Vodka will evaporate more quickly and make the surface less sticky, so if you use water, make sure you don't use too much. Aim to evenly dampen the surface of the fondant so that it is tacky, but not wet. Leave it for 1–2 minutes, then dab off any excess stickiness using a paper towel.

Take a gold leaf on its backing paper and gently but firmly smooth it against the dampened area. Pull away the backing paper and move onto the next section. Repeat across the cake, overlapping the edges of the gold leaf slightly, until the sides and top of the cake are covered. Do not touch the gold once you pull the backing paper away as it will break and crack while it is still setting.

You need to leave the gold leaf to dry, ideally overnight. Once everything has dried, take the large fluffy brush (a brand new, clean blusher brush is ideal) and very gently buff away any excess gold leaf. Pay particular attention to the joins that were overlapped and the top and bottom cake edges, as the majority of the excess gold leaf will be found at the joins.

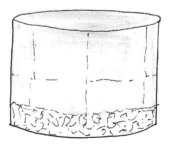

Gold leaf
celebration cake

BRUSH-EMBROIDERED LACE

Taking a classic technique that has been used on wedding cakes for years and playing with the colour palette gives this cake a sophisticated fashion feel. Or stick to ivory and pastel shades for an elegant bridal cake. The brush embroidery takes a little practise, but it is pretty forgiving as it disguises wobbly piping, and you can pipe over any mistakes along the way.

prepared cake

20-cm (8-in) round layered cake, filled, crumb coated and covered in a smooth layer of mauve fondant (see pages 10–25 for guidance)

lace decoration

Yellow food colouring paste
½ batch Royal Icing (see page 16)
Vodka or water

Add a small amount of yellow food colouring paste to the royal icing and mix well until combined and you have the colour you want. Add 1–2 drops of water so that the royal icing has a soft peak consistency. Place the icing in a piping bag and cut a small hole that has a diameter of 1–3 mm (¹/₁₆–¹/₈ in) across the tip. Alternatively, fit the piping bag with a very small plain tip.

You can use the lace-design template on page 157 for this project, adding some of your own leaves or flowers if you feel there are gaps in the design that you would like to fill. Alternatively, you can design your own pattern and work with that, tracing and indenting your own design as described here.

Using a sheet of parchment paper and a pencil, trace your enlargement of the lace template shown on page 157.

Now follow the steps on page 133 to begin the brush-embroidery technique. Repeat these steps for the leaves and other flowers. Don't be tempted to pipe more than one outline at a time as the royal icing will start to dry and you won't be able to blend it smoothly.

Yellow lace flowers on mauve fondant

BRUSH EMBROIDERY TECHNIQUE

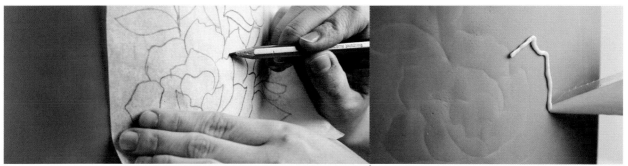

1 Gently hold the tracing against the side of the cake and retrace it using a sharp pencil to leave an indentation in the fondant. Do not press too hard as you will leave finger indentations and the pencil will pierce the paper. Any mistakes can be corrected as you're piping or by adding in a leaf here and there. (You can, of course, indent a design freehand using a cocktail stick or a kebab stick if you feel confident.) Repeat the tracing around the sides and top of the cake until you have a staggered repeat that is evenly spaced out across the cake.

2 If you wish, you can practise the brush embroidery technique on the template before working on the cake itself. Pipe a line from a petal on the outer edges of the flower design.

3 Dampen the paintbrush by dipping it into vodka or water and press off any excess liquid. While the royal icing line is still wet, carefully pull the icing in stripes toward the inner part of the petal with the tip of the paintbrush to fill the petal area.

4 Pipe the outline of the next petal that sits towards the outer edges of the flower design and drag the icing in towards the centre in the same way. Work your way around the flower edges so that the outline is filled out before moving inwards to the next layer of petals and then, finally, to the centre of the design.

CUT IT OUT

For a modern, clean feel, a cut-out design is ideal. This is a simple pattern to practise this decoration technique, but once you've mastered it, try your own designs. Remember that fine details are difficult to cut out and make the fondant fragile, so keep your design bold and simple.

prepared cake

20-cm (8-in) round layered cake, filled, crumb coated and covered in a smooth layer of fondant (see pages 10–25 for guidance)

cut-out decoration

400 g (14 oz) ready-to-use white fondant
400 g (14 oz) white gumpaste
Food colouring paste
Icing sugar, for dusting
Vegetable fat
Vodka or water

Measure the height and circumference of the prepared cake and cut two identical long strips of parchment paper that will each wrap all the way around the cake and that match the cake height exactly. On one strip, trace the outline of the template on page 157 using a pencil.

Knead together the fondant and gumpaste until the mixture is smooth and pliable. Now knead in a little food colouring paste until you achieve the colour you want.

Dust your work surface with icing sugar. Using a large nonstick rolling pin, roll out the fondant to a thickness of approximately 3 mm (1/8 in) so that it is large enough to cover one of your parchment paper strips. Lightly grease the plain parchment paper strip and place the fondant over the top, smoothing it into place with your hands. Trim the fondant to the size of the paper.

Place the traced design onto the rolled-out fondant and align the edges. Lightly re-trace the design with a pencil to create an indentation in the fondant that you can use as a cutting guide.

Remove the template and, using a clean scalpel, cut away the areas of the design marked out by the indentations. You'll need to work fairly quickly to avoid the fondant drying out too much, which is why a simple design is ideal to start with.

Using a small (food-only) paintbrush, dampen the fondant cut out with a little vodka or water. Lift the fondant cut-out on the parchment paper backing and gently press it against the sides of the cake. Start at one end and slowly wrap the fondant sleeve around the cake until the other end joins up. This seam will be at the back of the cake.

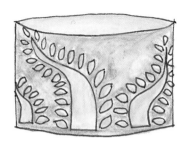

Blue cutout design on green fondant

Once attached, start to peel away the parchment paper from the design. Hold the fondant strip in place if necessary until set. Smooth it with your hands to ensure it has adhered everywhere. It is not really possible to move the fondant strip if you get the placement wrong, so be confident and make sure you have the measurements correct at the start.

Trim off any excess fondant at the join. If the fondant extends above the edge of the cake, carefully trim off the excess by running the scalpel carefully along the edge of the cake.

MARIE ANTOINETTE

Marie Antoinette would most certainly have approved of this lady-like and pretty cake. Swags, roses and pearls in a soft colour palette of blush pink and teal create a cake that has lots of classic charm and a touch of decadence.

prepared cake

20-cm (8-in) round layered cake, filled, crumb coated and covered in a smooth layer of fondant (see pages 10–25 for guidance)

swag, rose & pearl decoration

250 g (9 oz) white gumpaste
Small amount of Simple Syrup (see page 17) or edible glue
250 g (9 oz) ready-to-use ivory fondant
Food colouring pastes
Edible pearl lustre dust

Fondant covered cake with gumpaste swags

First, make the swags. Measure the circumference of the cake and divide the total by 5 to ascertain how far apart the swags should be spaced. Mark a little indentation on the cake with the tip of a knife at each interval.

Tint a chunk of gumpaste using colouring paste, if desired, and roll it out to a thickness of 3 mm (1/8 in) in a rectangular shape. With a sharp knife, cut out a rectangle that is approximately 15 x 8 cm (6 x 3¼ in). Gather together the rectangle so that it is loosely pleated and pinch the ends together. Brush a little edible glue on the ends and along the back, then drape the swag on the cake between two of the marked points, pressing at the ends first before gently fixing along the length of the swag. If it starts to slide, hold it in place a little longer or add a bit more glue. Repeat for the remaining four swags using the rest of the gumpaste.

To make the rosettes, tint a chunk of fondant using colouring paste. Roll it out to a thickness of 3 mm (1/8 in). Using a 3-cm (1¼-in) round pastry cutter, cut out five circles. Use a 2-cm (¾-in) round cutter to cut out five more circles. Thin and frill the edges using a frilling tool (see page 123) until ruffled. Apply a small amount of edible glue or syrup to the back of a larger disc in the middle, leaving a gap around the edges. Attach this to the side of the cake at the point at which two swags join. Add a smaller disc to the middle in the same way, then tease the frilled edges with your fingertips to emphasise the ruffles. Repeat to make four more rosettes, one at a time, and apply them to the cake to cover all the swag joins.

Using fondant, follow the directions on page 96 to make pearls of a uniform size and decorate them in pearl lustre. Roll twenty-five small pearls and attach five of these to the centre of each ruffled rosette.

Brush a little edible glue around the bottom edge of the cake in a band shape. To attach two to three rows of pearls, start at the bottom and work all around the cake, them move up to the next row.

MERINGUE DROPS

These spiky little meringue drops look wonderful all over a cake, lending it fantastic three-dimensional texture as well as colour. The meringues are delicious, so you'd be forgiven for munching on them as you decorate!

prepared cake

20-cm (8-in) round layered cake, filled, crumb coated and covered in a smooth layer of buttercream (see pages 10–25 for guidance)

meringue drops

300 g (10½ oz) pasteurised egg whites or 9 egg whites
300 g (10½ oz) caster sugar
300 g (10½ oz) icing sugar, sieved
3 tbsp freeze-dried strawberry fruit powder
3 tbsp freeze-dried blackberry fruit powder
Food colouring pastes in pink and purple

frosting

¼ batch Classic Buttercream (see page 14)

Berry flavoured meringue

To make the meringue drops, preheat the oven to 100°C (215°F).

Start whisking the egg whites in the large bowl of an electric stand mixer set to a low speed until foamy, then increase the speed to high. When you reach the medium-firm peak stage, start adding the caster sugar by the spoonful while whisking on a medium speed. When the mixture is firm and glossy, gently fold in the icing sugar until combined.

Divide the meringue mixture between two large bowls and fold one of the fruit powders into each portion, along with the corresponding food colouring paste, until you have two streaked meringue colours.

Line some baking trays with parchment paper. Spoon each of the meringue mixtures into a piping bag and cut a large hole that's approximately 2 cm (¾ in) wide into each tip, or fit each bag with a large plain tip. Pipe blobs of meringue that are approximately 5 cm (2 in) in diameter onto the lined baking trays.

Bake for 2 hours, then turn off the oven and leave the meringues inside with the oven door propped ajar until they are cool.

To decorate the cake, spoon the buttercream frosting into a piping bag and cut a large hole that is approximately 1.5 cm (⅝ in) wide into the tip or fit the bag with a large plain tip. Pipe a dot of buttercream onto the back of a meringue drop and attach it to the side of the cake at the bottom. Repeat with another meringue drop, attaching it beside the first one. Repeat around the cake until you have completed one horizontal row, then move up to the next row, attaching meringue drops directly above those in the first row. Continue in this way to cover the sides, then attach more meringue drops to the top of the cake until the entire cake is covered. Allow the buttercream to set for 30 minutes.

NAKED

Take delicious looking bare cakes, stack them together, and you get a fabulous centrepiece full of rustic charm. The crumb coating helps to keep moisture in, as totally naked cakes dry out faster when on display. Make each tier individually and dowel them for support (see below), then assemble the tiers directly onto a cake stand, only when at the venue, for freshness and stability.

prepared cakes

2 x 20-cm (8-in) round cakes, each cut into 2 layers, then filled and stacked to make 1 cake of 4 layers (see pages 10–25 for guidance)
2 x 15-cm (6-in) round cakes, each cut into 2 layers, then filled and stacked to make 1 cake of 4 layers (see pages 10–25 for guidance)

frosting & decoration

1 batch Classic Buttercream (see page 14) or Italian Meringue Buttercream (see page 14)
Fresh flowers and/or berries (make sure the flowers are food safe and pesticide free)

Dowelled cake stack

Stacked cakes require dowelling for stability and to stop the tiers from squashing the ones below. The dowels help to disperse the weight of the cake between the dowels and the rigid cake board. You'll need five standard plastic dowels for this project, which you can purchase from any good craft cake decorating store.

Put each of your two layered cakes onto a cake board of the same size – a little smear of buttercream will hold them in place. Next, apply a thin coating of buttercream as you would a crumb coat (see pages 22–23), scraping off the excess buttercream to reveal some of the cake layers here and there, which is the look that gives this naked cake its name.

As this cake has only two tiers, you'll need to dowel only the lower 20-cm (8-in) tier. Take a clean 15-cm (6-in) cake tin and place it centrally on the top of the cake. Lightly trace around the edge of the cake tin with the tip of a knife. This tells you how big the tier above will be and marks its positioning on the cake.

Take the dowels and mark positions for them on the top of the cake, spacing them about 3.5 cm ($1^3/_8$ in) in from the traced line, and also evenly apart from each other. Push the dowels down into the cake at the marked positions, keeping them upright, until they hit the cake board. Using a pencil, mark each dowel at the point at which it comes out of the cake so that you can cut it at that point to make sure that the dowel is flush with the top of the cake when it is inserted into it.

Carefully pull out the dowels and line them up next to each other. Holding them firmly in place, cut them to the same length with a serrated knife, finding the average point of all your pencil marks as a cutting-point

guide. Make sure the dowels are of exactly the same length. This will ensure the cake stacks level. Use sandpaper to file down some of the ends if necessary – just wash the dowels afterwards. Re-insert the dowels into the cake so that it is ready for the next tier.

Once you have a cake stand ready where your tier cake will be displayed, stack the tiers. Naked cake is less robust than a fondant-covered cake, so it is better to not move it once stacked. Place the bottom tier onto the cake stand and spread a little buttercream onto the middle of the top using an angled metal spatula. This will help to glue the tiers together a little, making the cake more stable. Lift the next tier onto the bottom tier, using an angled metal spatula to help lower it and the traced outline to help position centrally.

Finally, scatter fresh flowers and/or berries between the tiers. You can use a little buttercream to fix some of the decorations in place if necessary. Make sure the berries are not freshly washed – they should be totally dry.

CHEVRON

Bold and graphic, this design is the perfect antidote to prettier cakes. It is put together in panels on each side of the cake, so you can master the technique on the first side and the remaining three panels will be super easy to create.

prepared cake

20-cm (8-in) square layered cake, filled, crumb coated and covered in a smooth layer of fondant (see pages 10–25 for guidance)

chevron decoration

300 g (10½ oz) ready-to-use white fondant
300 g (10½ oz) white gumpaste
Food colouring pastes in 3 colours
Icing sugar, for dusting
Vodka or water

Measure one side of your cake and cut a piece of parchment paper to the same size.

Knead the fondant and gumpaste together until smooth and pliable. Divide the mixture into three equal portions and knead a small amount of food colour paste into each portion.

Divide each colour into four portions and wrap three portions of each colour tightly in cling film, reserving a portion of each colour to use right away.

Dust your work surface with icing sugar. Using a large nonstick rolling pin, roll out the tinted fondants to a thickness of 3 mm (⅛ in). You are aiming for long strips that are 9 cm (3½ in) wide and as long as the width of one side of your cake and the sheet of the parchment paper you cut (which should be around 21 cm/8¼ in).

Now it's time to create three chevron strips to decorate one side of your cake. To do this, you'll need a 4-cm (1½-in) square pastry cutter. Follow the instructions on page 145 to cut the three rolled fondant strips into the correct shapes.

To decorate one side of your cake, brush the fondant chevrons with a little vodka or water to dampen them.

Lift up the parchment paper along with the chevron panel on it and press the panel against one side of the cake, fixing it in place.

Repeat the rolling, cutting and decorating process with the remaining portions of tinted fondant.

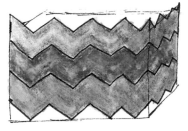

Coloured fondant chevrons

143

MAKING FONDANT CHEVRON PANELS

1 Turn the square cutter so that it looks like a diamond shape. Line up the two opposing corners to the sides of this diamond shape with one long edge of the fondant strip and cut out a triangle. Cut triangles along the edge, side by side, so that a zigzag edge forms. Repeat with one long edge of each of the other two fondant strips.

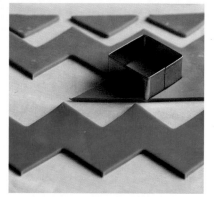

2 Cut out triangles along the opposite uncut edge of each strip in the same way, shifting the cutter along so that the point of it is in the centre beneath each joining triangle above. This creates the chevron pattern. Allow to set for 30 minutes.

3 Lightly grease the sheet of parchment paper and carefully lift the chevrons onto it, tucking the points of one strip into the recesses of the strip above it. How you lay them out on the paper is how they will appear on the side of the cake, so take your time to get the positioning right.

CHOCOLATE INDULGENCE

Wave upon wave of rich, dark chocolate is punctuated by coordinating roses dusted in gold, which have the effect of catching light and also intensify the dark tone and texture of the chocolate. This statement cake is a chocolate lover's dream! Its free-form texture is very forgiving to the impatient cake decorator.

prepared cake

20-cm (8-in) round layered cake, filled, crumb coated and covered in a smooth layer of ganache (see pages 10–25 for guidance)

chocolate decoration

725 g (1 lb 10 oz) dark chocolate chips (minimum 53 per cent cocoa solids) or, if using a block, chopped finely
500 ml (17 fl oz) glucose syrup
Icing sugar, for dusting
Edible gold lustre dust

Make the modelling chocolate in advance. Put 625 g (1 lb 6 oz) of the chocolate into a heatproof glass or ceramic bowl. Melt the chocolate in the microwave in short bursts (or use the double-boiler method – see page 66.) Heat until just melted. Place the glucose syrup in a separate bowl and heat to roughly the same temperature as the chocolate. Pour the syrup into the melted chocolate and stir well until completely combined. Allow to cool.

Once the mixture is completely cool, transfer it to a piece of cling film and wrap it tightly. Leave to set overnight at room temperature.

When you are ready to make the fans and roses, peel away the cling film from the modelling chocolate and knead it until it is smooth and pliable. It will be quite hard to start with, so if you are having trouble, cut it into smaller pieces to knead it, or heat it for very short bursts in the microwave and then continue to knead.

Cut a chunk off from the block of modelling chocolate that is the size of a lemon. Dust your work surface with icing sugar. Using a nonstick rolling pin, roll out the chunk of modelling chocolate to a thickness of 3 mm (1/8 in). Using a sharp knife, cut out rectangles that are approximately 20 x 10 cm (8 x 4 in) in size.

Gather together a rectangle to create a pleated effect, then pinch the pleats together on one of the long edges to create a fan shape. Pull apart the top part so that it is wider and more defined. Repeat with the remaining rectangles of modelling chocolate.

To make the roses, use the remaining modelling chocolate and follow the instructions for making roses on page 95.

Chocolate waves with gold roses

When you are almost ready to decorate the cake, pop it into the fridge to chill for 30 minutes, which will speed up the amount of time it takes for the decorations to stick later on.

When you are ready to decorate the cake, put the remaining dark chocolate chips into a heatproof glass or ceramic bowl and melt in the microwave in short bursts (or use the double-boiler method – see page 66). Allow to cool until thickened but still smooth. Place the melted chocolate in a piping bag and cut a 3-mm ($1/8$-in) hole across the tip, or fit the bag with a plain tip.

Using a medium (food-only) paintbrush, dust the fans and roses with gold lustre dust. Brush off any excess dust.

Pipe a small amount of the melted chocolate onto the back of a fan and fix it onto the cake. You may need to hold the decoration against the cake until the melted chocolate sets. Repeat with the remaining fans. Now attach the roses with melted chocolate, positioning them in between the fans to fill any gaps.

MINI JEWELLERY BOXES

These chic miniature box cakes in iconic pale blue are ideal for celebrating an engagement in style. Change the colour for birthday party gift boxes. Stack them high on a cake stand and you have a sophisticated party talking point.

sponge cakes

1 batch Ultimate Sponge Cake batter (see page 11), flavoured with 1 tsp vanilla extract, or any recipe of your choice

frosting & decoration

1 batch Classic Buttercream (see page 14) or Italian Meringue Buttercream (see page 14)
Food colouring paste
1.25 kg (2 lb 12 oz) ready-to-use white fondant
Icing sugar, for dusting
Edible glue

Preheat the oven to 160°C (325°F). Grease and line a 20-cm (8-in) square cake tin. Pour the cake batter into the cake tin and spread it out. Bake for 45–50 minutes.

Level the top of the cooled cake using a large serrated knife or cake leveller, then cut the cake in half horizontally to create two layers.

Spread an even layer of frosting on one cake layer and sandwich the other layer on top.

Using a large serrated knife, divide the cake into sixteen squares that each measure 5 x 5 cm (2 x 2 in).

You'll need sixteen thin 5-cm (2-in) square mini cake cards for this project. Using a small palette knife, smear a little buttercream onto each cake card, then press a cake cube onto each card.

Cover each mini cake cube with a thin layer of buttercream. Chill in the fridge for 15 minutes.

Knead a small amount of food colouring paste into 1 kg (2 lb 4 oz) of the fondant. Break off a chunk of the tinted fondant and wrap up the remaining tinted fondant tightly in cling film. Ensure the white (untinted) fondant is also wrapped tightly and put it to one side.

Follow the steps on page 150 to decorate the cakes with the fondant icing. Make sure that each time you roll out some fondant, you do so on a clean surface dusted with icing sugar, and that you use a nonstick rolling pin.

Fondant covered mini sponges

JEWELLERY BOXES DECORATION

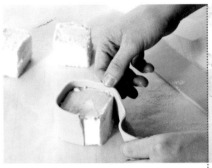

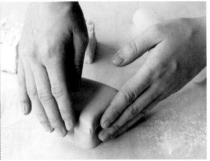

1 Roll out the tinted fondant to a thickness of 3 mm (¹/₈ in). Cut out a 25 x 5-cm (10 x 2-in) strip. Wrap the strip around a cake. Trim off the excess where the two ends meet using a sharp knife to make a neat join. Trim the fondant to the size of the cake at the top. Repeat until all cake cubes are wrapped in fondant.

2 Roll out some more tinted fondant and cut out sixteen squares that measure 8 x 8 cm (3¼ x 3¼ in) for the lids. Cut out a little 1-cm (½-in) square from each corner of each lid.

3 Place a lid on top of a cake and smooth the flaps over the edges, gently bringing the corners together to make a neat box shape. Repeat the process with the remaining lids and cakes.

4 To make the ribbons, roll out the white fondant to a thickness of 3 mm (¹/₈ in). Cut out thirty-two ribbons that measure 20 x 1 cm (8 x ½ in). Brush a little edible glue onto the back of the ribbons and attach two to each cake, overlapping one another to make a cross on top of the box. Trim off excess with a sharp knife at the bottom edges.

5 To make the bows, cut out another thirty-two ribbons that measure 10 x 1 cm (4 x ½ in) and sixteen ribbons that measure 5 x 1 cm (2 x ½ in).

6 Follow the instructions on page 83 to make sixteen miniature bows. Attach one bow to the top of each cake using a small amount of edible glue.

PARTY TIME

I have gone for a playful and very colourful design for this cake that's ideal for a birthday party. For a really special occasion, like a quinceañara or a wedding, a fabulous display of multiple cakes, with this one at the centre, looks stunning.

prepared cakes

20-cm (8-in) round cake, layered, filled, crumb coated and covered in purple-tinted fondant (see pages 10–25 for guidance)

15-cm (6-in) round cake, layered, filled, crumb coated and covered in green-tinted fondant (see pages 10–25 for guidance)

decoration

½ batch Royal Icing (see page 16), prepared to soft peak consistency

1 kg (4 lb 4 oz) ready-to-use white fondant

Food colouring pastes in purple, green, blue and pink

Icing sugar

Vodka or water

ultimate birthday cake

First, prepare the lower tier. It should be sitting on a cake board of the same size. Apply a small amount of royal icing to the centre of the board and position the 20-cm (8-in) cake onto it.

Take 300 g (10½ oz) of the fondant and, using food colouring paste, tint it purple to match the colour of the fondant covering the larger cake. Divide the remaining 700 g (1 lb 9 oz) into three equal portions. Tint one portion green to match the smaller cake, one portion blue and one portion pink.

Spread 1 tbsp of royal icing onto the centre of a 23-cm (9-in) base board and place the bottom tier in the middle. Dust your work surface with icing sugar. Using a large nonstick rolling pin, roll out a long strip of the purple fondant to a thickness of 3 mm (⅛ in). Aim for a length of approximately 70 cm (27½ in) and a width of 3 cm (1¼ in). Brush a little vodka or water onto the exposed cake board and carefully lift the fondant strip around the circumference of the base board to cover it. With a sharp knife, cut the fondant where the ends meet at the back to make a neat join and trim off the excess fondant around the board. Knead the scraps of purple fondant together and cover with cling film to use later.

Dust your work surface with icing sugar. Roll out each colour to a thickness of 3 mm (⅛ in). Cut out four strips of each colour, each of which are 2.5 cm (1 in) wide and long enough to extend up the side of the cake and over the edge.

Apply a small amount of vodka or water to the back of one strip using a clean paintbrush. Attach the strip to the side of the cake vertically, smoothing it from the bottom edge upwards, and over the top edge toward the centre. Cut off any excess fondant that extends beyond the middle of the top with a sharp knife. Repeat this process, alternating colours as you work around the cake. Allow to set for a couple of hours. Now decorate the top tier. Put 1 tbsp of the royal icing into a bowl, cover

it in cling film and put it to one side. Tint the remaining royal icing using food colouring paste. For the cake in this picture I've used purple, to match the lower tier. Put it into a piping bag. Cut a small hole that measures approximately 3 mm (¹⁄₈ in) wide across the tip, or fit the bag with a small plain tip. You'll use this for the swags on the top tier. Follow the instructions on page 154 to pipe the swags. Leave to set for 1 hour.

You'll need four plastic dowels to assemble the tiers. Dowel the bottom tier following the instructions on pages 140–141. Spread the middle of the bottom tier with the reserved plain royal icing and place the smaller tier on top, using a medium angled metal spatula as a lifting aid.

Roll the remaining tinted fondant into little balls with a diameter of approximately 1 cm (½ in). Using vodka or water, stick these around the bottom edge of the top tier, alternating colours as you work around the cake.

Finish off with a posy of fresh flowers on top or a number cake topper.

PIPING SWAGS IN ROYAL ICING

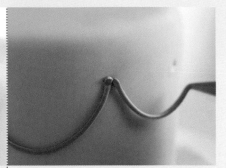

1 Measure the circumference of the cake and divide the total by 5 to ascertain how far apart each swag should be placed. Mark a little indentation on the cake with the tip of a knife at each measured interval. (The mark will be covered by the swags later on.)

2 Hold the tip of the piping bag against one starting point and gently squeeze so that a little royal icing makes contact with the cake.

3 Maintaining a steady pressure, lift the bag away in a sweeping motion to join the string of icing to the next mark. Allow gravity to form the swag shape. Do not touch the cake at all (apart from at the first and last point for each swag). Don't worry if the string breaks – just scrape it off, clean off excess icing with vodka and start again.

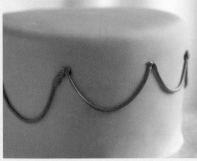

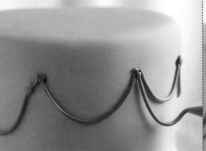

4 Repeat these piped swags, alternating the length for a varied effect. Alternating them in this way is very forgiving as you don't have to try to make them all with the same length of drop.

5 Add another row of swags beneath the first set.

6 Pipe little loops at the top of each join to neaten the overlap.

TEMPLATES

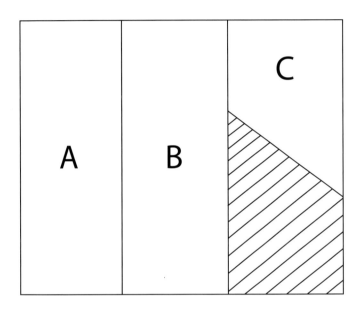

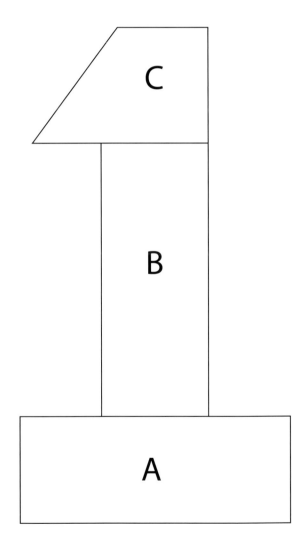

COUNT TO TEN Use the cutting guide (above) and the positioning guide (right) to make the cake project shown on pages 114–115.

CUT IT OUT Copy this template at 145 per cent to make the cake project shown on pages 134–135.

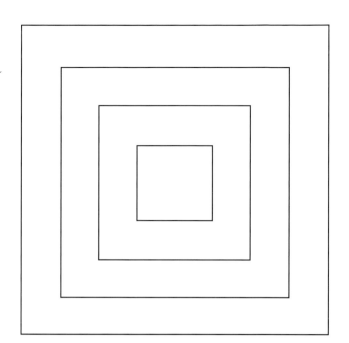

CUBIST COOL Use this cutting and positioning guide to make the cake project shown on pages 60–63.

BRUSH-EMBROIDERED LACE Copy this template at 165 per cent to make the cake project shown on pages 130–131.

INDEX

index

ACKNOWLEDGEMENTS

The beautiful photographs in this book were taken by two very talented photographers who brought alive the ideas that had been brewing in my mind for months and gave me the boost needed to carry on through long days of shooting: Clare Winfield, partner in crime, who I am now proud to call my friend; and Ria Osborne, who is never afraid to start making a bit of bunting out of thin air and power through challenges.

Amazingly, Salima Hirani has managed to make the editing of this book one of the most enjoyable parts. Editor and project manager extraordinaire, she has been a constant source of comfort and reassurance, dishing out confidence boosters and constructive pointers at every step. The fantastic book that you hold in your hands wouldn't be what it is without Salima.

I wouldn't have taken the leap into this layer cake adventure were it not for the unending encouragement from my family: the daily phone calls to my mum, talking through ideas, and her complete belief in me, were a lifeline; my love, Chris, who has endured more mess in the kitchen than most, and not complained. His daily support and love has given me the strength to do more than I thought I was capable of. And I am very grateful to my friends for being so understanding as I disappeared to do this project, I think I owe them a lot of cake as thanks.

ABOUT THE AUTHOR

Ceri Olofson is a master cake designer and owner of acclaimed London-based cake studio Olofson Design. A leader in her field, Ceri has developed a reputation for exquisitely designed wedding cakes. Her creations are regularly featured in the international press, including *Brides* and *Wedding Cakes: A Design Source* magazines.

Ceri began baking at an early age, influenced by the patisseries from her childhood spent in France. By the age of 15, she already had a recipe binder of her own tried and tested baked treats, many of which she still uses to this day. After training in the fine arts and gaining a degree from the University of the Arts in London, her passion for baking and her creative eye inevitably collided. Learning sugarcraft from the ground up, she has developed a practical approach to cake decoration and enjoys creating designs using accessible tools and ingredients.